Praise for *Seeding Innovation*

"In *Seeding Innovation*, Robyn charts a practical and heartfelt call-to-action for leaders who are eager to build something better—for the planet, for our food system, and for themselves. Robyn is one of those unique people who sees possibility and works to build bridges (not divisiveness) between people to solve our biggest problems. And, she brings her authentic self to this book—it's grounded in courage and faith—and I think it's the perfect guide at the perfect time from a true thought-leader."

—**Steve Young**
Managing Partner, Manna Tree Partners, a private equity
firm focused on improving human health through nutrition

"Women have always been the backbone of society, culture, and the economy. That reality is finally getting the recognition it deserves in the twenty-first century, with women leading businesses and organizations that not only outperform their male peers, but also inspire the next generation of *all* people. . . . *Seeding Innovation* is a must-read for anyone who wants to better understand the opportunities that lay in front of us and to claim their role in this seismic shift."

—**Erin Gallagher**
CEO and Founder of Ella,
Fast Company's World's Most Innovative Recipient

"Finally, a book, *Seeding Innovation*, that creates a real guide for practical and tangible innovation and change from the old, outdated limited measurements of GDP and capitalism. Robyn paves the way through her brilliance and expertise to help create a new and expanded lens of how we move forward here and now, together with greater purpose and impact in business and how we live on this planet."

—**Darin Olien**
Author and Emmy Award Winning Host of
Down to Earth with Zac Efron

"What does advice for entrepreneurs look like when the markets, the investors, the services and products are changing before your eyes? How do we shed the orthodoxy of the existing, failing system? Well, the answer is you dig deep, you move from the linear simplistic mindset and into a circular, holistic one that embraces complexity in all its forms.

Robyn's personal journey, her wisdom acquired though years of wanting to be the change she wanted to see is reflected in this book. It's holistic in its eloquent framing of the macro business environment in poly crisis world (Planetary Boundaries, Economic, Political, and Social). It explains why ESG, DE&I, and personal work is central to building resilient, profitable businesses. *Seeding Innovation* presents both sober and practical tools for entrepreneurs and leaders wanting to create lasting value for people and the planet."

—**Erik Bruun Bindslev**
Global Impact Leader and Entrepreneur

SEEDING INNOVATION

THE PATH TO PROFIT AND PURPOSE
IN THE 21ST CENTURY

ROBYN O'BRIEN

WILEY

Published by John Wiley & Sons, Inc., Hoboken, New Jersey.
Published simultaneously in Canada.

For general information on our other products and services or for technical support, please contact our Customer Care Department within the United States at (800) 762-2974, outside the United States at (317) 572-3993 or fax (317) 572-4002.

Wiley also publishes its books in a variety of electronic formats. Some content that appears in print may not be available in electronic formats. For more information about Wiley products, visit our web site at www.wiley.com.

Library of Congress Cataloging-in-Publication Data:

Names: O'Brien, Robyn, author.
Title: Seeding innovation : the path to profit and purpose in the 21st century/Robyn O'Brien.
Description: First edition. | Hoboken, New Jersey : Wiley, [2024] | Includes index.
Identifiers: LCCN 2023057809 (print) | LCCN 2023057810 (ebook) | ISBN 9781394227105 (cloth) | ISBN 9781394227129 (adobe pdf) | ISBN 9781394227112 (epub)
Subjects: LCSH: Leadership. | Business planning. | Personnel management. | Organizational change.
Classification: LCC HD57.7 .O2688 2024 (print) | LCC HD57.7 (ebook) | DDC 658.4/092—dc23/eng/20240116
LC record available at https://lccn.loc.gov/2023057809
LC ebook record available at https://lccn.loc.gov/2023057810

Cover Design: Wiley
Cover Image: © oscar tang/Shutterstock
Author Photo: Darcy Sherman of Sassafras Photography
SKY10069360_031224

Dedicated to my four incredible children,
Lexi, Colin, John, and Tory

Contents

Author's Note

Dear Reader,

If you have this book in your hands, you've decided to be part of the solution. Thank you.

There are so many titles this book could have had: *Atomic Courage*, *A Smarter Future*, *Creating Solutions*, *Catalysts for Change*, *Informed Leadership*.

In *Silent Spring*, Rachel Carson warned us what would happen if we didn't address our toxic systems. The World Bank recently did the same in a report called "Detox Development: Repurposing Environmentally Harmful Subsidies." The data shared in *Seeding Innovation, The Path to Profit and Purpose in the Twenty-first Century* proves Carson's words true, with the help of entrepreneurs, innovators, thought leaders, the World Bank, and other asset managers. It also highlights the important role that women and whistleblowers play when it comes to change. As our clean air, clean water, clean soil, and biodiversity are depleted, we find ourselves in deep need of a diverse array of talents and innovative skill sets. As the European Central Bank shares, nature and our economies depend on it.

In April 2023, I was meeting with a friend who shared his concern about the world his kids are inheriting. I said, "Someone needs to write a business leadership book on best practices that protect our kids' futures and the planet, that inspires people to participate in the solutions."

Two days later, an email appeared in my inbox from a senior editor at Wiley Publishing: "Hello Robyn. My name is Brian. I'm Sr. Editor at Wiley publishing. I'd love to connect as I'm eager to know if you might have some interest in writing a book on how businesses can better implement sustainability practices, eliminate waste, etc. I'd love to connect and to discuss in more detail if you might have some interest."

If that isn't the universe responding, I don't know what is.

The day I received his email, my youngest child had just turned 18. I was about to have an "empty nest." I'd spent two decades raising four children, while working in the food and finance industries, founding everything from nonprofits to financial service firms, all aimed at making clean and safe food affordable and accessible to anyone who wants it. To me, food security is a national security issue. I'd worked on these issues since my kids were little. I'd taken them to meetings with investors, members of Congress, to events at the State Capitol, and into product testing kitchens. I wanted them to understand that love is an action and that action is an antidote to despair.

In meetings, I watched as food and finance executives struggled with integrating meaningful, long-term change, whether that was around equity, diversity and inclusion efforts, environmental stewardship, conservation, or impact. I heard from countless investors and entrepreneurs, and I could still sense the fear and uncertainty in the capital markets. The industry hadn't fully mobilized.

There is clearly a hunger for change, solutions, and the courage needed to create them. I feel the demand for it every time I give a keynote. People are in search of inspiration and purpose and so hungry to be fueled by passion and courage.

I am fascinated by courage. It's something I developed early in my career, as the only woman on a team that managed $20 billion in assets, in an industry that is 98% white and male. We were a team of seven, and the guys asked me to cover the food industry. So I learned the operating models, the financials, which leadership teams were trustworthy, and which teams made me want to wash my hands after a meeting. I sat in on tech meetings to learn more. I wanted to not only understand what made a resilient business model, but also what made a resilient leader. I listened and learned.

When my youngest child suffered a life-threatening allergic reaction, I was called to display a courage I didn't know I had. I challenged the multinational food and chemical companies over their double standards, spoke out on price-gouging by the pharmaceutical companies, and found myself in situations where courage wasn't even a choice because staying silent was far riskier than any concern of speaking out. But courage also didn't come naturally. I had to learn how to be brave, how to find my voice, build a team, inspire a movement, again and again, and I found that a lot of people were asking for *that*: show me how I can be braver in my life.

What makes us brave? What holds us back? And what is it about fear and failure that keeps us playing small when we know something bigger like innovation and change need to happen?

I used to think that courage is the opposite of fear. I was wrong.

In fear, there is a sense of scarcity, that we may fail, that we may be abandoned and rejected. And so we convince ourselves that if we stay small, we can avoid the pain, discomfort, fear, and possibility of rejection.

Only it doesn't quite work that way. Because, when you abandon your potential and dreams, you essentially reject yourself, the truth of who you are, your hopes, dreams, and capabilities in order to play small. And *that* is the ultimate rejection. A rejection of your purest potential. You risk drowning under the weight of "what ifs" and what could have been.

But rarely can you just flip a switch and turn on courage. It usually isn't that easy. Courage is like a muscle, and the more you use it, the stronger it gets. It's also contagious and will inspire others to be courageous too.

I am not going to go into a long list of everything that ails us right now on this planet that we share. There are daily headlines about it. If our debt levels are any indicator, it's clear that we are living beyond our means. We've got some huge environmental issues confronting us, but that also means that there is enormous opportunity to get involved and create solutions.

It is a brave thing to stand up in business (and life) and say, "You know what? This is intolerable. Enough. There has to be something better." And to go about figuring out what that is and how to make it happen. Innovation and change won't happen without courage. Courage is at its core.

So how do you find the courage to take an idea and turn it into something? A product, a company, a movement, a campaign? What is required to move something from an idea that hits you in the shower to something that you put on a spreadsheet and then build a team and a company around? Because it is so clear that the world, all that we are facing, needs inspired, almost atomic, innovation and courage.

In *Seeding Innovation*, you will learn not only the mechanics of building out a business, but also how to embrace an attitude of curiosity over judgment and wonder over blame. You will learn how to take action steps, and with deep humility and honesty, explore and challenge the beliefs, patterns, relationships, and behaviors that are holding you back. You will encounter naysayers and nonbelievers. Many people, maybe even those closest to you, will want you to stay where you are, to play small, because you are more predictable there. And you will have a choice: to stay or to move forward toward your calling.

A calling is exactly that, a call, with a chance to answer it or decline it.

Answering that calling to innovate and to drive change in a world that values conformity and sameness is one of the bravest things you can do. It sets in motion a series of events that you may not yet see, challenges for which you don't yet have answers, and possibilities that are unfathomable. But if you feel that calling inside of you, to do something more, create something new, build something better, get really quiet and figure out how to answer it. Because the day we abandon our dreams, decline that call, is the day that we give up on ourselves.

So fear? Fear of rejection? Fear of failure? Fear is going to ride shotgun to innovation most of the way. Instead of running from it, you will learn how to embrace it, as the familiar friend that it is, and learn how to work with it and move through it. I will ask you to take inventory of your fears, so that you understand them, and as you do that, to also consider and weigh the deep fear of regret.

I will ask you to consider who you surround yourself with on this Journey (and it's a journey with a capital "J"), to investigate how homogenous that group currently is, and if that homogeneity creates a blind spot. We will take inventory on that too.

And there will be plenty of times that you will be tested. A lot of the work of an entrepreneur has nothing to do with the company you are building or the product you are creating. It has everything to do with what's going on in your head, what is happening between your ears. Resiliency is a critical resource, and self-awareness is an asset.

We will address how you talk to yourself. We will get to work on changing that internal dialogue, the criticism and even self-loathing, and identify the media and noise that is fueling the negativity that you've carried around for too long. Because those hidden fears—the voice in your head and its incessant chatter—can self-sabotage and shackle you to past behavior. The negativity, feeding yourself those thoughts, won't serve you as you move forward. It's like trying to *not* eat junk food while keeping a bunch of junk in your head. It doesn't work. We've got to clean out the junk. So we are going to get really brave and take inventory of that too.

I will share data to motivate you and stories to inspire you. You will hear from entrepreneurs who were homeless, sleeping on the floor of the San Francisco airport, who are now running multimillion dollar venture funds. You will hear from entrepreneurs who failed forward, out of the trunk of their cars into adding Rihanna and Jay-Z to their cap tables. And you will hear from entrepreneurs who revolutionized how we think about everything from water to investors.

All of these friends created something that helps move us forward, making people's lives better and meets us where we are as humans, addressing our fundamental need to be seen, heard, and loved. And all of them, in their darkest moments, leaned into a purpose that was greater than themselves to help propel them forward. I'll help you discover what that is too.

And through all of this, you'll develop your "FQ score"—your unique power and purpose.

I think that's why this entrepreneurial journey of innovation and the lessons that accompany it are so rewarding, because of how fundamentally human it is with its mistakes and imperfections, its learning curve and humility, its self-discovery and growth.

Innovation is the hero's journey, and if ever there was a time for heroes for our planet, that time is now. Thank you so much for answering that call to do something. I am here to support you, with resources, data, inspiration, and tools, because I've learned it is way easier to do this work when someone has your back. Let's get going.

—**Robyn**

1

Blind Spots and Big Opportunities

"There is nothing in a caterpillar that tells you it's going to be a butterfly."
—R. Buckminster Fuller

FAULT LINES ARE emerging in business as we know it, and paradigm blindness is catching a lot of companies off guard.

For those innovating, creating, and designing, the opportunity couldn't be bigger. You only need to look to the auto industry to understand how quickly change is happening, as the car industry electrifies to decarbonize road transportation.

But what gives innovation life? What turns an idea into a successful business model? Most of us have hundreds of ideas every day, but how do we get an idea out of our head and into action?

It has as much to do with mindset as it has to do with access to capital. It has as much to do with the structure of our belief systems and how we handle setbacks as it has to do with the structure of our balance sheets and how we handle the competition. And it has as much to do with how we respond to imposter syndrome and naysayers as it has to do with how we treat our team and employees.

If you're launching a business, a new product, or service, you'll confront all of this. My goal is to not only help you to seed innovation, but also to do it successfully, which means there is a lot to cover, so let's get started.

From the Shower to the Spreadsheet

If you ask entrepreneurs what happened to them when their idea cut loose in their brain, they'll tell you it took on a creative life of its own. It became an obsession. We all have ideas. So many of them. But what makes us act on them? To write them down? What makes us brave enough to share them with someone? And keep working on them in the face of remarkable odds?

Nolan Bushnell, cofounder of Atari, said, "Everyone who has taken a shower has had an idea. But it's the people who get out of the shower, towel off, and do something about it that makes the difference."

An idea that motivates you so much that it inspires you to take action. An idea that makes inhibition, fear, rejection, even ridicule and derision tolerable. Why do some people give their ideas life while others leave them tucked away in their minds? Why do some unshackle an idea and let it run, while others bury it?

How does a concept become reality? And how do you get an idea from the shower to a spreadsheet? Anyone can dream about building the Empire State Building, but how do you actually do it?

Ideas shape the course of history.

—John Maynard Keynes

There is an obsession with entrepreneurship. And wrapped around that obsession, you will find courage and naysayers, scaffolding, and failed ideas. You will find heartache and joy, monumental mistakes, and wild successes. You will find cheerleaders and support systems, and you will find dark nights of the soul.

When you were a kid, you probably had something that you obsessed over. Maybe it was cars, or baseball cards, BMX bikes, stickers, or unicorns. You collected them; you were all in. People knew you for it. You lived and breathed it. It was probably your first obsession. Mine? A collection of Coca-Cola cans from around the world, in varying sizes and shapes with different languages on them. I was fascinated by the ability of one brand to create universal awareness across hundreds of languages with its colors and fonts. I loved collecting them.

The passion, focus, and obsession in entrepreneurship is similar to that of the unbridled passion of a child. You lock in and can't *not* think about it, you can't not do it. When someone suggests that you do something else, it's as if they're asking you not to breathe or to unplug your heart. It's not an option.

Something makes you step out of the shower and into building out your idea, and you begin to live its creations, and life gets singular really fast. There is a fierce focus and courage, and a willingness to face fear, other people's opinions, and society's conditioning in order to make way for creativity and innovation.

Which may be why so many ideas fail to launch, because it requires so much of us psychologically, physically, emotionally, and even spiritually.

Too often, business leadership books only focus on the financial aspects of starting a business, the operational aspects, the team building, and the logistics. But what about the headspace of the entrepreneur? The internal dialogue? The ongoing criticism? Their support system? Their lack of one? How often is faith challenged when an entrepreneur is pushed to an unimaginable pain point? How often has imposter syndrome sabotaged more ideas than lack of funding?

The recipe for entrepreneurship contains all of this, and courage could not be more important.

We need innovation—new, collaborative ideas, and smarter business models, and we need courage to execute them.

Why? Because we are staring down some pretty sizable problems, and it's clear that business as usual isn't going to cut it. In fact, none of the world's top industries would be profitable if they paid for the natural capital they use. In a sobering report (TRUCOST, 2013), the world's biggest industries burn through $7.3 trillion worth of *free* natural capital a year. And it's the *only* reason they turn a profit.

Only it's not free, we're paying a very steep price for it.

So what is "natural capital"? Things like clean air, clear water, healthy soils, the basic things we need to survive. Think of them as "nature's capital." They aren't on balance sheets, but every company on the planet depends on them, as does every person. So when a company burns through them, pollutes them, and destroys this natural capital, it's called "externalized costs." These are the costs not paid for by a business but by society at large. For example, a corporation that pollutes local water sources with the spraying of its chemicals is externalizing the costs on to whoever drinks that water and whoever has to clean it up.

The concept of "externalities" is becoming increasingly familiar in business, from boardrooms to investors. Many first learned of this concept through the tobacco industry, when it became clear that smoking cigarettes causes cancer. The industry profited while people got sick. We then learned about it in agriculture, when lawsuits around the world linked glyphosate, a chemical sprayed onto food crops, to cancer. And we are learning about externalized costs imposed by the fossil fuel industry on all of us. It isn't just human health that's impacted by these externalities, though the cost there is massive and merits its own book; it's the health of the planet and those we share it with too. And it's presenting a liability to business as we know it.

Somewhere along the way, we forgot or ignored that we actually need the planet to survive. All business depends on natural capital.

According to Ceres, a sustainability advocacy nonprofit, and Lyon et al. (2018), 94% of S&P 100 companies acknowledge the science of climate change and 93% consider it a material risk factor, but almost 30% lobbied against some policies that would help address it. Think about that for a minute—there is almost complete consensus among all of the companies on the S&P 100 that climate change presents a material risk factor to business, and yet almost a third of those companies lobbied against policies that would help address it. It's corporate suicide.

So why is it so hard for companies to change?

How Paradigm Blindness Costs You

One might argue that it's paradigm blindness.

According to Adam Smith in *Powers of the Mind*, a paradigm is a shared set of *assumed* facts.

In *Discovering the Future, the Business of Paradigms* (1993), Joel Arthur Barker goes further by suggesting that paradigm blindness is "a set of rules that define limits and establish what is necessary to be successful within those limits."

But what happens when we exceed the limits? Things either break or change.

In the 1930s, there was an inventor named Chester Carlson. He'd developed a new system made of black powder, iron, wax paper, and a steel plate, along with a few other things, like cat fur. He reached out to IBM, Kodak, and more than 40 other companies with his new idea and was rejected by all of them.

Except one, a company called Haloid Photographic Company. No one understood Carlson's vision, except Haloid, who would not only develop it but also go on to change the company's name to Xerox, after the wild success of Carlson's creation (Bermúdez, 2023).

Too often in business (and life), someone sharing a new idea is met with the response, "That's not the way we do it here." Or "If you had my experience, you'd know that wouldn't work." Or even more condescending: "Good luck with *that*." It's why inventors like Sara Blakely of Spanx share how important it is to keep your concept and new idea close for the first year. Not so much to protect the concept, but to protect your determination to see it through.

Rarely is something visionary seen or understood as visionary by many at the start. Why? Because it is so far outside of the status quo. It challenges conformity and stands to disrupt so much. Few have the audacity to dream that it can be done, even fewer the sheer determination to see it through.

One of my absolutely favorite terms to describe entrepreneurship is "creative destruction." It was coined by Joseph Schumpeter, and I first learned about it in business school. It was one of those moments when it felt like something in my brain exploded, a total a-ha moment. It made complete sense. We've all lived it too.

For those of us that walked around with Sony Walkmans, we could never have imagined CDs, much less streaming devices like Spotify, but each company disrupted the one that preceded it, making it obsolete. We used to wear wristwatches; now we carry smartphones and wear small computers on our wrists. Creative destruction is innovation.

Rebooting Fiduciary Duty

In *Beautiful Economics*, a handbook for rebooting the world with a new economic narrative that combines ecological, philosophical, and entrepreneurial wisdom, Howard Collinge writes, "In our current economic model, humans are one-dimensional units in a giant mathematical equation. If the equation leads to bigger and bigger

Gross Domestic Product (GDP), higher share prices, and more cars, the economy is doing fine. (But) something doesn't quite add up."

Collinge goes on to write, "GDP is the measure of all consumption, but it does not distinguish between good or bad consumption or take into consideration the long-term consequences and possible environmental damage."

Our obsession with growth and GDP has been "catastrophically short-sighted."

Business to date has focused on growth at all costs. It's the "fiduciary duty" of business leaders to drive shareholder return. Some call it cutthroat capitalism, some call it dog eat dog, and some call it business as usual. But the next generation is flat out calling it out, as the externalized costs, discrimination, and injustice become obvious. It's their future at risk, and they're demanding better not only from the governments, but also from the companies they both buy from and work for.

As my friend, Paul Hawken, author of *Blessed Unrest, Natural Capitalism, Regeneration, Drawdown*, and so many thought provoking books, says: "We are stealing the future, selling it in the present, and calling it 'GDP.'" It's extractive capitalism.

If one business is mindful of its impact on the planet, while another burns down forests, isn't one creating more value than the other? And won't that impact market share? Employee retention? Recruiting? And should that factor into share price and even its role in GDP?

Soil holds more than 25% of all biodiversity and provides 95% to 99% of food to 8 billion people (Joint Research Centre, 2022). If a company destroys soil, should its contribution to GDP be discounted, compared to a company that protects natural resources? If a company destroys soil with their products, should they be held accountable? Is that product not only a liability on their balance sheet, but also a liability to an economy dependent on biodiversity?

In February 1937, President Franklin D. Roosevelt, the 32nd president of the United States, wrote to all state governors: "The nation that destroys its soil destroys itself." He understood decades ago that business is dependent on nature.

I don't know a single company or business that doesn't source the food its employees consume from the soil. Business, all business, across all industries, play a role here. And many are starting to figure that out. From Patagonia to Bayer, from AI to NGOs, you're either part of the solution or part of the problem.

And fancy press releases, virtue signaling, and box ticking aren't going to cut it. Asset managers and investors are demanding more, consumers are demanding more, and employees are demanding more.

Business has to move to meaningful action to mitigate risk and capture market share. We can't just use the word "sustainability"; we have to become it. We can no longer abuse the environment we depend on; we have to regenerate and protect it. So what to do?

We all have a role to play. Increasingly, an important role is the role of the *chief sustainability officer*. As Robert Eccles and Alison Taylor (2023) wrote:

> The role of the chief sustainability officer (CSO) is undergoing a rapid and dramatic transformation. Historically CSOs have acted like stealth PR executives—their primary task was to tell an appealing story about corporate sustainability initiatives to the company's many stakeholders, and their implicit goal was to deflect reputational risk. The role had virtually no involvement in setting company strategy or communicating it to shareholders; those responsibilities fell to the CEO, the CFO, and the head of investor relations.
>
> Now, however, some CSOs have moved away from a role centered on messaging and instead are spearheading the true integration of material ESG (environmental, social, and

governance) issues into corporate strategy. This pivotal change requires close collaboration with other members of the senior leadership team and active engagement with investors . . . . By integrating sustainability initiatives with risk and governance, CSOs can effectively tackle this conflicting messaging, address growing concerns over hypocrisy, and ensure that sustainability programs do not merely serve as a cover for shortcomings in ethics and governance.

I thought of my friend, Karen Fang, the CSO at Bank of America, when I read this article. She integrates ESG principles into her work, particularly in the food industry. She is focused on transitioning the supply chains of multinational food companies to regenerative agriculture. Why? It mitigates climate risk, which can drive profitability. It takes intelligent leadership against an entrenched status quo to drive change at this level, but a powerful CSO can play an incredible operating role in a company's profitability if their recommendations are followed, and they demonstrate the financial impact of both action and inaction.

So how do we motivate long-term behavior change?

Plenty of books and articles can tell you what not to do, to chastise. But shame is one of the hardest emotions, and while it may motivate short-term behavior change, it can also shut people down and create a defensiveness. What child responds well to that? And the truth is that there is a child in all of us. So how to inspire the change?

There will be lawsuits, litigation, policy change, and more. But how do we motivate a business leader to bravely move forward? How do we motivate an entrepreneur to take the risks necessary to step into innovation? It's been demonstrated over and over again that positive reinforcement serves as a much better motivational tool.

So my goal is to reframe this challenge as an opportunity, to give examples, showcase business models designed for the twenty-first century, and to offer suggestions of things that you can do—things that you can add to your business plan, your model, in order to build a business that you are proud of, one that is flourishing in market share and employee retention and happiness.

What we need is a diversity of creative thinkers, innovators, and problem solvers obsessed with developing smarter models, models that don't degenerate our limited resources like clean air, clean water, and healthy soil, but rather, business models that regenerate them. We need both entrepreneurs and *intrepreneurs* (which are employees looking for ways to innovate and improve their work inside of a company) who are obsessed with driving change. And we need to also address the ridicule and derision, the naysayers and the nonbelievers that often accompany this kind of innovation.

Creative Destruction's ROI

A great example of the ridicule that can accompany innovation is the story of Netflix.

I witnessed the Netflix story firsthand when I was sitting on the trading desk at Invesco (formerly AIM) when Blockbuster went public. Blockbuster's IPO valued the company at $465 million. The company had 100% market share. They were the movie rental king with 9,000 stores and 60,000 employees. It was the way we watched videos.

Which is what makes the story of Netflix so fascinating.

Netflix started in the late 1990s with a subscription model that had no due dates and no late fees when it came to renting videos, and the company was growing like crazy during the internet boom. It was such a fascinating time to be an investor, with companies like eBay also going public. At the time, I was meeting visionary founders like Pierre Omidyar and his newly hired CEO, Meg Whitman.

But then all of a sudden, the internet bubble burst, and as Marc Randolph, the cofounder of Netflix, and others share, where the .com at the end of a name had been a badge of honor, it was now three scarlet letters. The company spent $50 million getting to that point, and according to Randolph, it began to look like the success was going to bankrupt them.

He shared on LinkedIn,

> The obvious strategic alternative for us was Blockbuster. Which is why, just a few weeks later, you found me, Reed (Hastings), and our CFO Barry McCarthy sitting at a giant conference table on the 37th floor of the Blockbuster head-quarters in Dallas, getting ready to pitch Blockbuster.
>
> The pitch was simple. We would join forces with Block-buster. We would run the online business. They would run the stores. We would jointly develop a blended model. And every-one would live happily ever after.
>
> And it was going great. They were leaning in. They asked good questions. Until they asked the most important question of all: "How much?"
>
> Now, we had rehearsed this. We figured we were $50 million in the hole . . . so let's go with that! Reed leaned forward con-fidently and told them: "Fifty Million Dollars."
>
> There was perfect silence. Their words were "we'll consider it," but we could tell they were fighting to suppress laughter. After that, the meeting went downhill fast.

Netflix was laughed out of the room. Can you imagine that car ride back to the airport or hotel? Either total silence or the face burning shame that is felt with rejection.

We all know how this story ends. Blockbuster had paradigm blindness. With 100% market share, they could not conceive of any other way beyond their existing store model. They'd set the rules (which were actually blinders), and Blockbuster's leadership lacked the vision, creativity, humility, and, importantly, diversity of opinions and perspectives that are essential to navigating change or to even considering a blended or hybrid model. Their blind spots were absolute.

And today, Netflix, the company that Blockbuster had the chance to purchase in 2000 for $50 million, has a market cap that exceeds $150 billion.

Blockbuster, afflicted with acute paradigm blindness, took itself out. Where the company once had 9,000 stores, it now has just one.

For the last decade, I've used this example in my keynotes to show the power of innovation, courage, and curiosity, as well as the risks of paradigm blindness. And as a reminder to always believe in the power of creative disruption, even against 100% market share.

So what's the lesson here? Systems change happens, paradigm blindness is dangerous, and innovation and entrepreneurship will always be working to tackle society's greatest challenges, to creatively build smarter.

Some attributes and characteristics are essential to navigating this kind of change: a tolerance for risk, fortitude, tenacity, humility, curiosity, a strong support system, and courage.

As my friend and *New York Times* best-selling author, Katherine Center, wrote, "You have to be brave with your life so that other people can be brave with theirs."

We are living in an era that our grandparents could not have fathomed and might only have called "atomic disruption." It's something I could not have imagined back on the trading desk in 2000 as the internet took shape. So much is changing so quickly that it can be hard to wrap our heads around it even now.

Today, we have artificial intelligence, ChatGPT, remote/robotic surgical procedures, lab-grown meats, drones, and climate technology, and the landscape of innovation and entrepreneurship is accelerating and wide open. According to Mike Thomas (2023), "Healthcare startups have embraced technologies like artificial intelligence, block-chain, and data analysis to disrupt inefficient processes of the past." Joyful Ventures, a fund started by my friend Jennifer Stojkovic, is a social impact fund focused on developing plant-based meat and protecting the environment. She's looked at hundreds of ideas this year alone.

Some ideas will stick, and the market will decide that some are dangerous. Innovation will continue, thank goodness, as the next generation demands accountability and change.

A Glassdoor for the Planet

So let's talk about the next generation, because right now, there are five generations working side by side. Understanding the needs of Gen Z is important not only because they are customers, but also because they are employees.

According to Deloitte (2023):

> Six in ten Gen Zs and millennials say they have felt anxious about the environment in the past month, and roughly the same percentage cite extreme weather events and wildfires as a stress driver. These concerns impact their decision-making, from family planning and home improvements, to what they eat and wear. Respondents are taking a range of actions, such as purchasing an electric vehicle or avoiding driving a car altogether, making their homes more energy-efficient, eating a vegetarian or vegan diet, and avoiding fast fashion in favor of second-hand clothes.
>
> Some are deciding to have fewer or no children to reduce their environmental impact. Climate concerns also play an important

role in Gen Z's and millennials' career decisions. More than half of respondents say they research a brand's environmental impact and policies before accepting a job, while notably, one in six say they have already changed jobs or sectors due to climate concerns, and around a quarter of respondents say they plan to do so in the future.

It's like a Glassdoor review of environmental and ethical practices.

In fact, the ability to drive change on social issues overall has the potential to make or break the recruitment and retention of these generations. According to Deloitte, "Nearly four in ten say they have rejected work assignments due to ethical concerns, while more than one-third have turned down employers that do not align with their values.

Gen Zs and millennials want their employers to help empower them and provide training and support, both to help them make more sustainable decisions in their own lives, and to develop the skills needed for the transition to a low-carbon economy."

This is not a luxury to younger generations of employees, clients, and customers. It's an absolute. Clover Hogan, the founder and executive director of Force of Nature, shares: "Today, 70% of young people today are eco-anxious; 56% believe that humanity is doomed." She's a very clear voice calling for action, and she is not alone. The data around anxiety and depression around younger generations doesn't lie. It's why I joined the board of directors for One Green Thing, a nonprofit organization that helps address these growing concerns and drive solutions. There is even a term for the anxiety and depression experienced as it relates to climate change: eco-anxiety.

According to Deloitte's study, it's estimated that approximately 800 million jobs are vulnerable to climate extremes.

I am not going to hammer on this fact. There are people who will say that climate change is a fabrication or has been happening for thousands of years, but Exxon speaks to the topic of climate change with incredible clarity and predicted it with incredible accuracy. Projections created internally by ExxonMobil starting in the late 1970s on the impact of fossil fuels on climate change were very accurate, even surpassing those of some academic and governmental scientists, according to an analysis in *Science* by a team of Harvard-led researchers. In "Assessing ExxonMobil's Global Warming Projections," researchers from Harvard and the Potsdam Institute for Climate Impact Research show for the first time the accuracy of previously unreported forecasts created by Exxon's scientists from 1977 through 2003. The Harvard team discovered that Exxon researchers created a series of remarkably reliable models and analyses projecting global warming from carbon dioxide emissions over the coming decades.

"What we found is that between 1977 and 2003, excellent scientists within Exxon modeled and predicted global warming with, frankly, shocking skill and accuracy only for the company to then spend the next couple of decades denying that very climate science . . . . We found that not only were their forecasts extremely skillful, but they were also often more skillful than forecasts made by independent academic and government scientists at the exact same time" (McCarthy, 2023).

So what did they choose to do about it once they knew what they'd created? Did they choose to invest in infrastructure change or more sustainable solutions? No, they chose to lobby and influence policy. According to Willam J. Snape, III, Assistant Dean, American University, Washington College of Law, 93% of Congress, close to 500 of its 535 members, has received funding from the fossil fuel industry. Why does this matter? Because lobbying influences policy, you can follow the money. But does it mitigate the environmental risks? Not at all, just the political ones. And do I expect the fossil fuel industry to attempt to discredit this data? Absolutely. But just a reminder, between 1977 and 2003, excellent scientists within Exxon modeled and predicted global warming with shocking skill and accuracy. It was an inside job.

And it left them wide open to the electrifying change we are now seeing in the auto industry, solar industry, and more. Rather than adapt and innovate, they lobbied and ignored the data.

As S&P 100 companies acknowledge the material risk of climate, and the evidence of the damage it's doing to the environment continues to mount (with industry-funded scientists now reaffirming it), integrating practices that reflect and protect the concerns of both younger generations and the planet into today's business models is nonnegotiable. It's a fiduciary responsibility.

Asset managers and investors are demanding it.

Because it turns out that most of us are increasingly allergic to destroying the planet that we depend on, whether its chemical pollution across our food supply, the destructiveness of fast fashion, extractive mining, discriminatory practices, the injustice of child labor, or all of the above, we have visibility into practices we couldn't see just one generation ago, thanks to new technologies and social media. And we talk about it. It can be challenging to bring up some of these issues in the boardroom and at the family dinner table, but ignorance is no longer an option, given the growing awareness of the damaging impact of the status quo.

Businesses built in the twentieth century may have failed to acknowledge externalized costs, but the transparency of the twenty-first century demands it. It's a liability to ignore them. Building business models mindful of the future, and their impact on people and the planet, not only mitigates risks, but it also ensures long term shareholder value, drives employee retention, and more.

Data are mounting that it's the best thing you can do to protect your long-term value and bottom line.

According to a McKinsey (2023) report, "Over the past century, global consumer consumption has been a central driver of economic prosperity and growth. This success, however, also comes with social and planetary impacts that result from producing, transporting, and discarding these consumer products. It should thus carry a moral imperative, for consumers and companies alike, to understand and address these impacts to society and the planet as part of buying decisions . . . . Product label claims—if they represent true and meaningful environmental and social action—can be an important part of fulfilling this moral imperative."

We see all kinds of innovations across categories and industries that are addressing this. It's not just consumers demanding transparency, but also employees and investors. A fellow executive producer on *Common Ground* is Ian Somerhalder. He's incredibly well known for his leading role on *Vampire Diaries*. But he and his wife, Nikki Read, are also very active in the environmental space. The more he learned about the food system's role in climate change, the more he wanted to create solutions, so he cofounded a bourbon brand called Brother's Bond. It couldn't be more timely. According to Bacardi Limited's annual trends report, 70% of North American consumers sought out sustainable or eco-friendly spirits brands at the end of 2020. Just as we are looking for better for you options in the grocery store, the same trend is happening in beverages. The name of the report is pretty telling, too: "From Domestic Hedonism to Mindful Moderation, the Bacardi Survey Reveals Spirits Trends Sparked by Cultural Shifts Last Year."

In an interview with Jillian Dara (2021), Ian Somerhalder and Paul Wesley said, "Building communities around farming and regenerative agriculture is the way to the future." Somerhalder explained that in the next decade there's an opportunity for a great change in agricultural practices as the existing generation passes control to a younger (and by proxy, more progressive-thinking) generation. "We see that as a very powerful and positive thing," he said. "The companies that are going to create the largest amount of stewardship are the companies with the triple bottom line: people, plant, profit."

The most important skillset a business leader today can have reflects the skills of a student: an openness and vulnerability to learn, a willingness to collaborate, a humility to acknowledge what you don't yet know, and a curiosity and courage to explore and learn more.

If we keep doing what we've done, in light of what we now know, and expect anything to change, that is the very definition of insanity. It will keep us locked in this abusive relationship with each other and the planet.

We have an enormous opportunity in front of us to build better.

We reinvent ourselves on a personal level often, taking up new activities, training for races, learning a new language, a new sport, a new instrument, and more.

The invitation is for business to do the same. We can't afford paradigm blindness on a planet with limited resources.

The Audacity of Vision

Professor Scott Galloway shared on his website, No Mercy No Malice, "A vision that's not widely derided likely isn't much of a vision."

I couldn't agree more. Plenty of people thought I was nuts when I first highlighted the level of corruption in our food system and began calling for transparency, change, and labeling back in 2008. Now, films like *Rotten*, *Poisoned*, *Common Ground*, and others echo and amplify this message around the world. What's nuts is to accept a status quo that we know is hurting us and our children.

Galloway went on to share, "MLK was a radical reformer who had a 63% disapproval rating at the height of his activism. Women were perceived as physically incapable of the demands of flight, until Amelia Earhart landed her Lockheed Vega in an Irish farmer's field."

Big visions are often called crazy and radical, but it's impossible to imagine a world without them.

When you were a kid, you thought anything was possible. Somehow cynicism and social conditioning take hold, a fear of failure sets in, and too often, conformity governs, and imagination and curiosity stop.

Curiosity allows you to explore. Imagination allows you to conceive—to both expand your thinking and produce new ideas, new visions, new concepts, new companies.

As Colleen Reilly (2023) shared, "Many adults find it easier to live as the expert who knows everything, rather than admit they don't know something or be the student who seeks knowledge."

And that's a grave mistake.

Some of the best advice I got as a young entrepreneur is "surround yourself with people who have talent and experience you don't have." A woven fabric is stronger than any one thread. In other words, know your vulnerabilities and build a team that is stronger than any one individual and especially stronger than any one demographic's lived experience.

When you do this, you will have to confront your ego (more on that later), and you'll have to get really good at listening (more on that too).

So as we head out on this journey together, my goal is to surround you with people who have experiences you don't yet have, to share their talents and expertise.

I invite you to listen with curiosity, not judgment, as we explore stories of both wild failures and wild successes, often within the same company. I will share the mindsets and the skillsets of those who succeeded and how they overcame seemingly impossible odds. Though, the word impossible, while often broken down into the cliché "I'm possible," is just really something that hasn't been done yet. The electric car was once impossible, as were streaming music, drones in agriculture, and surgical procedures conducted by robots. Few could have imagined the gamification of farming that is occurring or so much of the innovation that we now access today. And even as I write this someone, somewhere, lies awake all night looking up at the ceiling with an idea that just can't be shaken.

This book is going to take you through the process. Along the way, you will hear "no" a lot. There will be plenty of naysayers on this journey and plenty of nonbelievers. Imposter syndrome will rear its head. The key is to expect all of it, anticipate it, and to go beyond it. When imposter syndrome and the naysayers pull up, think, "Well, there you are," and welcome them in for what they are: a starting point.

Because more often than not, that "no" and that rejection will be a rerouting that will take you on an exceptional journey.

The Courage to Change

Why am I calling for courage? Because change can be hard. It is also happening at an accelerating speed, and that asks a lot of us. We see it in technology, with AI and Web3, we see it in our food system, and we see it in everything from health care to finance to politics. It can be both exhilarating and terrifying. Either way, it presents tremendous opportunities.

But what makes some people step toward the opportunities, while others shy away from them? It has as much to do with mindset as it does to do with capital.

I've been early to spot trends, and I've helped multinational companies, consumers, and investors navigate fault lines and transitions. I've found the courage to call out change and the data that supports it, which in some cases, put a target on my back.

I expect the same here, as the data I am about to share tells a story.

You can identify those leading change by the number of arrows in their backs, because leadership is often accompanied by a tsunami of naysayers. Change disrupts the status quo

I've found that more often than not, when the naysayers are trying to hold you down, you have a choice: you can either get pulled down by that energy or you can use that energy to propel you forward. I call it "the slingshot theory" and now anticipate the slingshot effect when driving solutions and change, and I've helped other leaders, executives, and policy makers do the same.

So this book isn't written for the naysayers. It's written for you, someone who is brave enough to examine the current situation, the status quo, the data, models, and infrastructure, to see the opportunities in them, to want to build something better, to create solutions, and to drive change.

Why? Because the systems we've inherited are failing us. They weren't designed for the twenty-first century and the unique challenges we now face. In almost every industry, there is an opportunity to drive innovation, profitability, and change.

Change happens when we are strong enough to admit that a problem exists. The data are telling us that there is a problem in everything from how we subsidize food and energy, to how we externalize costs, to how we generate artificial intelligence. The data are also telling us that there is everything from higher returns to higher productivity when we choose to address these issues and create solutions and challenge conformity.

Companies that manage their carbon emissions and mitigate climate change enjoy 67% higher returns than companies that refuse to disclose their emissions, according to CDP's Climate Action and Profitability Study (Lovins, 2023).

According to Gallup, an engaged workforce can give you up to 24% higher productivity and 21% higher profitability.

A Boston Consulting Group study of 1,700 companies in eight countries found that companies with above-average total diversity had both 19% higher innovation revenues and 9% higher EBIT margins, on average.

These numbers are material, and any board would be thrilled to see them. They come from an article written by my friend, Hunter Lovins, called "Integrated Bottom Line." Is it any wonder, despite a vocal group of naysayers, that "the vast majority of executives (92%) plan to increase their ESG (which stands for environmental, social, governance) data spend by at least 10%, with 18% planning an increase of 50% or more," according to Bloomberg's "ESG Data Acquisition and Management Survey" from March 2023?

ESG has become a lightning rod and quickly, but is it a valid metric?

As Lynn Forester de Rothschild, founder of the Council for Inclusive Capitalism, shared, "Acronyms tend to take on a life of their own, especially in the finance world." She thinks this acronym, ESG, should go away. "Still," she added, "the principles behind it are more important than ever. We need to lose the term I believe, and double down on the objective" (Goodkind, 2023).

It's very Shakespearean. A rose by any other name is still a rose, isn't it? So how do we embed the principles into business to drive higher productivity, higher returns, higher margins, and perhaps importantly, what happens if we don't?

The demand for enhanced ESG disclosure is intense. Globally, overall ESG investing is massive, having grown as much as tenfold in the last decade. Morningstar, Inc. estimated that total assets in ESG designated funds totaled more than US$3.9 trillion at the end of September 2021. This number, like the label, will wax and wane with the markets, but the principles are critical.

According to Bloomberg Professional Services (2023), "Environmental, Social, and Governance (ESG) labeled funds hold approximately $7 trillion in assets according to Bloomberg's analysis of 14,500 funds with ESG called out in their prospectus. A threshold indicating that this sector has achieved mainstream status. Despite this, the sector still has much work to do to overcome the challenges it was designed to tackle such as limiting global warming and creating more equitable corporate governance practices, among others."

In our increasingly polarized world, the ESG label has taken a politicized hit, but the returns on these principles are material, and they extend far beyond the bottom line.

According to Deloitte's 2023 Gen Z and Millennial Survey, "More than half of respondents say they research a brand's environmental impact and policies before accepting a job, while notably, one in six say they have already changed jobs or sectors due to climate concerns and around a quarter of respondents say they plan to do so in the future." Trying to attract the best talent and build out a strong team? This matters.

A group of 32 asset managers and investors managing $7.3 trillion in assets recently urged the G20 (a group of 20 of the world's largest economies) to link their financial support to the agricultural sector with their environmental obligations.

And by 2030, American women are expected to control much of the $30 trillion in financial assets that baby boomers will possess—a potential wealth transfer of such magnitude that it approaches the annual GDP of the United States (Baghai, Howard, Prakash, and Zucker, 2023).

The landscape of business is going through seismic shifts, and the data are mounting on the risks and opportunities these changes present to business as we know it. Investors want smarter business models, as it becomes increasingly clear that business as usual—its governance, externalized costs, and homogeneity—is a liability.

The United Nations (UN News, 2021) states that around 87% of the $540 billion in total annual subsidies to agricultural producers included measures that were price distorting and potentially harmful to nature and human health. In other words, we are funding our own destruction, according to the UN. In addition, a landmark report from the UK government (2021) revealed subsidies caused $4 trillion to $6 trillion in damage to nature each year.

"Annual investment in nature needs to triple to around USD $400 billion to successfully tackle the interlinked climate, biodiversity, and land degradation crises," according to the UN Environment Program (UNEP) State of Finance for Nature 2021 report.

But nature is competing with novel technologies that promise higher returns, so where can we find the $400 billion needed?

The World Bank in 2023 called for a "detox" of subsidies, totaling over $7.25 trillion a year, that are causing environmental harm (Carrington, 2023).

The World Bank refers to it as "detox development" and is calling for a shift in what we subsidize. This is not Greenpeace calling for change; it's the World Bank, the United Nations, and asset managers and investors. Why? Because this degradation is impacting bottom lines.

Calls to action are growing. We are waking up to, or perhaps remembering, the fact that "Humanity needs nature to survive" according to Frank Elderson (2023).

"Bank Boardrooms Need More Experts on Nature-Related Risks," read one Bloomberg headline (Bullard, 2023).

It's not just banks and investors who are now demanding change. Young people are demanding better products, more representation, and better, more inclusive values in the workplace, too. They are turning away from the jobs and golden handcuffs used to recruit prior generations (Miller, 2023).

Global asset managers and the next generation are not messing around. A paradigm shift is happening, and to mistake it as a trend or a fad is dangerous. I've spoken at Bloomberg, Morgan Stanley, and with banks, private equity firms, and impact investors.

Investors are demanding more responsible practices, and companies are scrambling, often putting a bandage (or a slick press release) over the problem, rather than going in and addressing the root cause. Investors are calling that out too.

"Investors warn 'fluffy' ESG Metrics are Being Gamed to Boost Bonuses," reads a headline in the *Financial Times* (Xiao and Temple-West, 2023).

This isn't a box-ticking exercise, a passing fad, or theme. "We need wholesale transformation of the food system, because it's one of the most-damaging systems of all to the climate and nature," said Rachel Crossley, head of stewardship for Europe at BNP Paribas Asset Management (Jessop, 2023).

But it's not just the food system that needs transforming—though that's been a focus of my career, and it's one of the first industries with supply chains impacted by our changing climate—it's business as we know it.

The auto industry is a powerful example of an industry going through electrifying change. A decade ago, electric vehicles were only 0.2% of new-car sales. By 2022, that number had grown to 13%.

Every day, from asset managers to whistleblowers, there are new calls to action. Investors along with the next generation of customers and employees are demanding better business practices.

These aren't radical activist groups; these are some of the world's leading financial institutions, not to mention the next generation of clients, customers, and employees.

It's not the first time we've been here.

We've experienced massive shifts in the ways we do business over the last 50 years, from Apple to Netflix, from ChatGPT and AI, to .com, .org, .edu, .io to fin+tech, ag+tech, climate+tech, and more.

Our entrepreneurial ecosystem could not be more important right now. Innovation is critical, and it demands vulnerability and courage.

Your mindset and support system need to be strong, so let's get going.

Action Steps: Inspiration Inventory

I want you to jot a few things down right now. Who inspires you? And why? They may be athletes, community leaders, coaches, entrepreneurs, musicians, artists, or others. Maybe it's family members or friends. They may be living or dead. Make a list of the people, places, things, ideas, and anything that inspires you. And hold on to it. You will be using this "Inspiration Inventory" later on.

Resources

Bacardi. (2021). *From domestic hedonism to mindful moderation, the Bacardi survey reveals spirits trends sparked by cultural shifts last year* [online]. Available at: https://www.bacardilimited.com/media/news-archive/from-domestic-hedonism-to-mindful-moderation-the-bacardi-survey-reveals-spirits-trends-sparked-by-cultural-shifts-last-year/

Baghai, P., Howard, O., Prakash, L., and Zucker, J. (2020). *Women as the next wave of growth in U.S. wealth management* [online]. McKinsey & Company. Available at: https://www.mckinsey.com/industries/financial-services/our-insights/women-as-the-next-wave-of-growth-in-us-wealth-management

Barker, J. A. (1993) *Discovering the future, the business of paradigms.* HarperBusiness.

Bermúdez, M. E. (2018). *Paradigms and the future of computing* [online]. Available at: https://slideplayer.com/slide/15068867/

Bloomberg Professional Services. (2023). ESG funds: What makes for good performance? [online]. Available at: https://www.bloomberg.com/professional/blog/esg-funds-what-makes-for-good-performance/

Bloomberg. (2023). *ESG Data Acquisition & Management Survey 2023* [online]. Available at: https://assets.bbhub.io/professional/sites/10/Bloomberg-ESG-Data-Acquisition-and-Management-Survey-2023.pdf

Bullard, N. (2023). Bank boardrooms need more experts on nature-related risks. *Bloomberg*.

Carrington, D. (2023, June 15). Vast fossil fuel and farming subsidies causing "environmental havoc." *Guardian* [online]. Available at: https://www.theguardian.com/environment/2023/jun/15/vast-fossil-fuel-and-farming-subsidies-causing-environmental-havoc-world-bank#:~:text=The%20%E2%80%9Ctoxic%E2%80%9D%20subsidies%20total%20at,are%20harmful%2C%20the%20bank%20says

Collinge, H. (2021). *Beautiful economics*. Simon & Schuster.

Dara, J. (2021). Ian Somerhalder and Paul Wesley discuss how their new bourbon supports regenerative agriculture. *Forbes* [online]. Available from: https://www.forbes.com/sites/jilliandara/2021/04/01/ian-somerhalder-and-paul-wesley-discuss-how-their-new-bourbon-supports-regenerative-agriculture/?sh=ecdd6b34aa08

Deloitte. (2023). *Deloitte's 2023 Gen Z and Millennial Survey reveals workplace progress despite new setbacks* [online]. Available at: https://www.deloitte.com/global/en/about/press-room/2023-gen-z-and-millenial-survey.html

Eccles, R. G. and Taylor, A. (2023). The evolving role of chief sustainability officers. *Harvard Business Review* [online]. Available at: https://hbr.org/2023/07/the-evolving-role-of-chief-sustainability-officers

Elderson, F. (2023). *The economy and banks need nature to survive* [online]. European Central Bank. Available at: https://www.ecb.europa.eu/press/blog/date/2023/html/ecb.blog230608~5cffb7c349.en.html

FAIRR. (2021). *The four labours of regenerative agriculture* [online]. Available at: https://www.fairr.org/resources/reports/regenerative-agriculture-four-labours

Goodkind, N. (2023). ESG has lost its meaning. One advocate says let's throw it in the trash. *CNN* [online]. Available at: https://www.cnn .com/2023/10/03/investing/premarket-stocks-trading/index.html

Jessop, S. (2023). Investor pressure group urges G20 to reform agricultural subsidies. *Reuters* [online]. Available at: https://www.reuters.com/ sustainability/investor-pressure-group-urges-g20-reform-agricultural-subsidies-2023-08-21/

Joint Research Centre. (2022). *Healthy soils, a necessity for the EU* [online]. EU Science Hub. Available at: https://joint-research-centre.ec.europa .eu/jrc-news-and-updates/healthy-soils-necessity-eu-2022-06-09_en

Lovins, H. L. (2023). *Integrated bottom line: A tool to quantify sustainable business performance* [online]. Available at: https://giteximpact.com/ 2023/05/25/integrated-bottom-line-a-tool-to-quantify-sustainable-business-performance/

Lyon, T. P., Delmas, M. A., Maxwell, J. W., Bansal, P. (Tima), Chiroleu-Assouline, M., Crifo, P., Durand, R., Gond, J.-P., King, A., Lenox, M., Toffel, M., Vogel, D., and Wijen, F. (2018). CSR needs CPR: Corporate sustainability and politics. *California Management Review*, 60(4), pp. 5–24. doi:https://doi.org/10.1177/0008125618778854.

McCarthy, A. (2023). Exxon scientists predicted global warming with "shocking skill and accuracy," Harvard researchers say. *Harvard Gazette* [online]. Available at: https://news.harvard.edu/gazette/story/2023/01/ harvard-led-analysis-finds-exxonmobil-internal-research-accurately-predicted-climate-change/#:~:text=The%20researchers%20 report%20that%20Exxon,would%20lead%20to%20dangerous%20 warming

McKinsey & Company. (2023). *Consumers care about sustainability—and back it up with their wallets* [online]. Available at: https://www.mckinsey .com/industries/consumer-packaged-goods/our-insights/consumers-care-about-sustainability-and-back-it-up-with-their-wallets

Miller, J. (2023, May 10). Big law firms fall out of fashion with idealistic Generation Z. *Financial Times* [online]. Available at: https://www.ft .com/content/c4c8a5fb-bee7-4e9a-81da-cb6255285619

Reilly, C. (2023). Are you curious about how this trait can increase innovation? *Forbes* [online]. Available at: https://www.forbes.com/sites/colleenreilly/2023/07/25/curiosity-and-innovation/?sh=b341116564aa

Smith, A. (1975). *Powers of the mind.* Random House.

Thomas, M. (2019). *25 healthcare technology companies that just might save your life someday* [online]. builtin. Available at: https://builtin.com/healthcare-technology/healthcare-technology-companies

TRUCOST. (2013). Natural capital at risk: The top 100 externalities of business [online]. Available at: http://naturalcapitalcoalition.org/wp-content/uploads/2016/07/Trucost-Nat-Cap-at-Risk-Final-Report-web.pdf

UN News. (2021). *Most agricultural funding distorts prices, harms environment: UN report.* [online] Available at: https://news.un.org/en/story/2021/09/1099792

UNEP, WEF, ELD, and Vivid Economics. (2021). *State of finance for nature 2021* [online]. Available at: https://www.unep.org/resources/state-finance-nature-2021

United Kingdom government. (2021). *The economics of biodiversity: The Dasgupta Review* [online]. Available at: https://assets.publishing.service.gov.uk/government/uploads/system/uploads/attachment_data/file/957629/Dasgupta_Review_-_Headline_Messages.pdf

Xiao, E. and Temple-West, P. (2023, August 27). Investors warn "fluffy" ESG metrics are being gamed to boost bonuses. *Financial Times* [online]. Available at: https://www.ft.com/content/25aed60d-1deb-4a41-8f39-00c92702b663

2

Finding Fearless Friends

"Once you make a decision, the universe conspires to make it happen."
—Ralph Waldo Emerson

EVERY ENTREPRENEUR YOU meet will tell you stories about people who tried to talk them out of their business idea. If they're honest, they probably remember the conversations in excruciating detail, the tone the person used, where they were standing or sitting at the time, perhaps even what they were wearing.

We remember it because of the emotions tied to it. We store negative information in our long-term memory much more quickly than it takes to store positive feedback (more on that later). Criticism and learning how to respond to it are part of the journey here.

So what's an entrepreneur with an unshakable idea to do with the naysayers and nonbelievers? When you are starting a business, you are going to find that there are plenty of them.

And if you surround yourself with naysayers, it will be shackling.

As Mathew Knowles (2023) wrote on LinkedIn, "When I started managing Destiny's Child, we had a great deal of non-believers around us, obstacles to overcome, rejections to face, and challenges to learn from . . . . [I]n your own endeavors, when you face the non-believers, obstacles, rejections, and challenges, it's important to know that when your foundation of belief is there and unshakable, that you can truly achieve anything you desire."

Beyonce's Renaissance World Tour grossed almost $600 million from 56 shows, grossing more than $20.1 million per night, now holding one of the records for the highest grossing single concert date in history. Imagine if her dad had listened to the early naysayers, and they had not had the belief system to overcome the early challenges and rejections?

It was Socrates who apparently said, "When the debate is lost, slander becomes the tool of the loser." It's a good thing to remember, but how do you build an unshakeable foundation? What happens when self-doubt inevitably creeps in?

Every entrepreneurial story includes naysayers. If we were creating a recipe for what entrepreneurship looks like—an ingredients list—naysayers and nonbelievers are going to be part of it. You can't avoid them, and I actually think they are required, like a test the universe gives you, to see how serious you are about your concept and how far you are willing to go, before things start to level up.

There are countless stories of rejection and ridicule that precede success, so how do you keep your vision and belief intact when people are telling you otherwise?

It comes down to what I've come to think of as our own supportive scaffolding—scaffolding that is of human design.

How to Design Your Scaffolding

When a new building is being constructed, or a gorgeous monument, scaffolding goes up around it as it is constructed. When you walk around any big city, scaffolding and supportive structures are everywhere.

The building of a business leader and entrepreneur is no different. We need support. If we are going to grow and become all that we are capable of as humans and leaders, we need supportive scaffolding around us, as this new version of us is constructed, the same way that a building or monument needs scaffolding when it's going up.

Entrepreneurship is very much the process of building something new and becoming something that hasn't existed before.

No two of us are the same, thank goodness. It's what makes innovation and entrepreneurship so exciting and unbridled. No two humans share the same experience. No two humans share the same skillset. No two humans share the same networks. The uncountable number of combinations of those three things alone makes entrepreneurship limitless. Perhaps that's why it is so fascinating, because anything is possible.

The mistake that too many entrepreneurs make is in trying to be like somebody else. And if you do that, you will ultimately fail.

For years, I've heard entrepreneurs pitch ideas saying, "We want to be the Patagonia of (fill in the blank)." They want to be "the Patagonia of the chip category," "the Patagonia of the kombucha category," "the Patagonia of the sausage category" (yes, it was a thing!). I heard it often when I worked with Rabobank and their Foodbytes innovation team. And while I appreciate the sincerity and simplicity in the analysis, I strongly encourage entrepreneurs to own their unique story and tell it with authenticity.

Why? Patagonia, by any measure, has been wildly successful, as a brand, a story, a leader, and as an influencer. But that success is part of the unique DNA and experience of the company and its founder, Yvon Chouinard, his wife Malinda, and their family. And if you've had the opportunity to meet Yvon Chouinard, you know why. He lives and breathes it. It's his obsession. When he walks into the room, you feel it. He's not wearing the flashiest new shoes, a fresh-pressed shirt, or crisp slacks. He doesn't have the latest gadget on his wrist. He's wearing something he's probably had for 30 years, a device is nowhere to be seen, and he will sit down with you, look you straight in the eye, and listen before saying anything, getting what feels like a soul read. He suffers no fools. He's seen plenty, and he's there to learn. It's the humility of a leader who understands that the world is always changing. He's both a teacher and a student.

What Yvon Chouinard had (and still has) when he started Patagonia was a passion and love for the outdoors. His mission? Protect the planet.

It's foundational to everything he does and how the company operates decades later. He doesn't pretend to have all of the answers, and he's willing to change his business model to reflect new information and stay true to his values.

It's a critically important trait of a strong leader: to realize that you don't have all of the answers. Chances are that the product idea that you have at the start of your business is rarely going to be the same one that you bring to market. There will be so many iterations. What you do have is a problem that you are trying to solve, something that you are doing that makes people's lives better. The product is going to change dozens if not hundreds of times. Curiosity is an important characteristic of a leader, and Chouinard has it.

What needs to be consistent are values that govern your work. Focus on that because that is where the mission comes from. It is what will attract the most aligned employees and help you build a strong team. It will send clear communications to your consumers.

And then focus on doing everything you can to develop an unshakeable belief that you will be able to figure it out, a belief that you will be able to learn, assemble, and gather the resources and team. You may have mountains of self-doubt inside your brain.

It won't serve you, other than to fuel fear. It's important to tackle that critical voice between our ears. Our subconscious hears every thought the conscious mind thinks. So how do we address the criticism in order to build an unshakable foundation?

It requires a level of self-awareness, knowing your strengths and weaknesses, and it also requires surrounding yourself with the right people and a multitalented team. And I'm not talking about yes-men or -women.

I'm talking about surrounding yourself with people who bring out the absolute best in you, the ones with whom you can safely brainstorm, the ones who are knowledgeable about not only market forces but also human behavior, the ones who share your name in rooms you're not in, and who have your back when you're not looking. The friends who are secure enough in themselves to reflect your highest self back at you, so that you don't play small. The friends who mirror your highest potential back to you. This is your supportive scaffolding, and it will be a stabilizing foundation and driving force in your success.

Building Your Supportive Scaffolding

Which reminds me of one of the very first times I met Alex Bogusky.

If you Google him, you will see that he founded one of the most successful ad agencies in the world, Crispin Porter Bogusky. He led award-winning campaigns and is now an incredibly successful investor.

But when I first met him, I didn't know any of that. I was introduced to him by a dear friend from college who worked with him at his ad agency. "You two need to get together," my college friend said. "You're talking about the same thing."

What thing? The absolutely messy state of our food system and what was happening to the health of our families.

I remember that first meeting so clearly. It was February 2010, almost a year after my first book, *The Unhealthy Truth: How Our Food Is Making Us Sick and What We Can Do About It*, came out, during one of the most isolating periods of my life. I'd challenged the multinational food and chemical companies over their double standards, calling out how they loaded the products they sold to Americans with artificial colors, high fructose corn syrup, and genetically engineered ingredients, pesticides, and ingredients that weren't allowed in their products in other countries. As I stepped forward into that work back in 2008, almost everyone I knew stepped back. It was a lonely spell, full of naysayers, bullying, and ridicule. I kept my head down and stayed focused. Back then, the existing paradigm was that our food system couldn't be *that* bad.

So I didn't take many meetings, the derision was so fierce, but I took this meeting as a favor to a friend.

That morning in February 2010, I tucked into a breakfast spot called Marie's. I was obsessively focused on how I was going to create a safer food supply and had barely looked up since the book was published in May 2009. I'd been almost entirely met with rejection, bullying, and people trying to talk me out of the work. "It can't be *that bad*, Robyn."

The nonbelievers in our broken food system were everywhere in 2010.

But I took the meeting.

And I found myself sitting in a booth with Alex Bogusky. We started talking about capitalism and Adam Smith. We talked about where we'd failed to learn certain things, assumed certain things, and where our systems were failing. I quickly found myself in a deep conversation with someone full of intellect and curiosity, a systems thinker, and our brains snapped together. At one point, he mentioned the Invisible Hand not being all that invisible, and he asked if I'd always thought outside the box. Curiosity was a characteristic I had as a child, it had earned me an early nickname, and when he said it, an unfamiliar sensation ran through me, and I looked across the table at him. He got it. I'd found a friend. In that moment, which I remember so clearly, it felt like something in me turned back on, a part of me that I'd let go quiet. Alex had studied human behavior in countless ways through his work in the advertising industry—what motivates us, what inspires us, what scares us. He understood systems change and social conditioning, and he'd challenged the tobacco industry in an award-winning campaign called "Truth."

The next thing I knew, his assistant walked in, encouraging him to leave, and as we stood up and said goodbye, I wasn't really sure what would happen next. Plenty of people had dismissed my efforts, plenty had been condescending, plenty had ridiculed. I remember looking him in the eye and thinking, "If nothing else, this was an amazing conversation."

So when I got back to my computer, I googled "Alex Bogusky." And out flew the results of his global ad agency, one that worked with clients like Domino's, Burger King, and others in the food industry, and my first thought was "Shit. Did I just get used for one of his campaigns? Was this guy just faking this?"

And almost at the exact time that I had the thought, an email appeared in my inbox from him, and it said something like, "Guess what? I just got back to the office, and we are pitching a new food company today. There is a giant box of mac and cheese in front of my office door."

And he wrote, "Insurgencies start from within."

I think about that line a lot. *Insurgencies start from within.* They drive change. For innovators, intrapreneurs, and entrepreneurs, that insurgency fuels the motivation, energy, and courage for fundraising, team building, creativity, and so much more. It takes on a life force of its own.

Oxford dictionary defines "insurgency" as "an active revolt or uprising." For example, "rebels are waging an armed insurgency to topple the monarchy."

For entrepreneurs, it is an insurgency against the status quo, the mediocrity, the injustice, the whitespace, the lack of access.

So by its very definition, entrepreneurship is an act of insurgency, a revolt against the status quo of the existing marketplace. To move forward, it is also an insurgency against the naysayers and nonbelievers, the voice in your head, and the fear that tells you to hold back because it's "safe." In order to take your idea forward, you will have to rise up against all of it. And doing that by yourself is a heavy lift. Because you aren't only dealing with the naysayers around you, you will also go toe to toe with the excuses you tell yourself. You will have to stand in front of the excuses, the nonbelievers, and you will have to push back on all of it.

When the first person understands you and sees you for it, when someone shares your belief in the mission and mirrors your potential back to you, it changes everything. For some, it may be a journalist covering the story; for others, it may be an investor willing to bet on you; for yet others, it may be finding a business partner or friend. But when you suddenly realize that you don't have to shoulder this vision entirely on your own, that other people see it too, that support is anchoring.

"I believe in you" changes everything, and it happened that morning over breakfast at Marie's.

Entrepreneurs can tell you how many rejections they received, and they will also remember that very first yes. It's why to this day, when I believe in someone, I love to be an early "yes," because I understand how lonely the road that precedes it is and the fortitude that is required.

When you first find someone who becomes part of your support system, that person doesn't have to agree with you completely; in fact, it's better if that person doesn't. But when someone truly sees you for who you are, what you are capable of, what you are trying to do and wants to see it accomplished too, it changes everything.

It needs to be someone you respect, like Alex, who will call you out when you try to play small, and who, when you waiver and start unloading excuses, will call you on that too because he (or she) finds it so unacceptable. Such people will mirror what is possible and reflect your highest potential back to you.

To make room for this kind of support also means that you will have to move the naysayers aside. If they are people who are close to you, that can be extremely hard. But a steady drip of negativity can kill passion and motivation faster than anything. You will have to make room for those who understand your ambition and purpose, the ones who understand that asking you to not do this is like asking you not to breathe.

The ones you choose to keep close will serve not only as scaffolding but also as encouragement, mentors, advisors, and inspiration, encouraging you to be the bravest version of yourself, a version that they can see that you may not yet be able to see or accept in yourself. They will mirror your potential back to you until you believe it yourself.

We see this play out often in the world of sports: a coach who champions a team with such an unwavering belief that the impossible becomes possible, whether it's Jason Sudeikis as Ted Lasso, or Deion Sanders, stepping in to build out the University of Colorado's football program. The coaching extends far beyond anything happening on the field and reaches deep into the hearts and minds of the players. As Deion Sanders often says, "You have to believe to succeed."

The same applications and practices happen in the building of a successful business team.

If you were to create a "diet" for an entrepreneur, encouragement would be one of the key ingredients. A steady diet of negativity can kill just about anything. Encouragement creates a sense of power.

And encouragement is a critical component to entrepreneurial success. If you break down the word, it has the word "courage" hiding in plain sight. Encouragement gives you the courage to push through some of your toughest times. The friends, relationships, and colleagues who are the supportive scaffolding around you are absolutely critical in the sea of naysayers and nonbelievers who will try to throw you off course. Those offering encouragement and counsel are the life raft that appears when you feel you are drowning in the enormity of the odds. They steady you when the winds of doubt blow strong. We see this over and over again in sports. The same applies in entrepreneurship. And ultimately, the most powerful relationships you have, both personally and professionally, will be those that elevate you to your highest potential, the ones who want to see you living at your fullest capacity. They are grounding, and they are precious.

And you will have a choice: to either listen to them or ignore them.

And I am telling you, it's not always easy or comfortable to listen to them. In fact, it's incredibly uncomfortable and unfamiliar in most cases. Because whatever dialogue you've got going in your head, it may have been running your entire life. You may have subconsciously (or even consciously) surrounded yourself with naysayers and people who amplify that internal negative voice because it is so familiar. So when someone challenges you and asks you to go beyond that internal narrative, your first thought might be, "Who are you to do this? And why should I listen to you?" Your inclination may be to find every reason and justification to not believe this person, to not listen to him or her, because it's so unfamiliar

The Big Risk in Playing Small

It happened the next time I saw Alex, which was probably about three months later. I'd given him a copy of my first book, *The Unhealthy Truth*, at that first meeting. When I saw him again, he had the book in front of him on the conference table at his office, a place called The Fearless Cottage. He said, "It's so good, but it's really annoying because you keep playing small. You kept saying you're 'just a mom' but you're so much more than that." He was really direct. "It's annoying," he said again.

I remember looking at him, thinking, "Who is this guy? And why in the world am I listening to this? I hardly know him." And I started thinking about all of the reasons why I needed to play it small.

But his words resonated. I was playing small. They resonated because I respected the work he'd done, especially challenging the tobacco industry in his "Truth" campaign. He was an early and courageous voice calling out the tactics of the tobacco industry. He'd stood in my shoes, which very few people had done. And he was right. I was playing small. I was playing it "safe." I didn't really want to be the one who was going to call out the food industry. Random House had published my book, I'd hoped that was enough, but companies were reaching out, people were paying attention, asking for more, so there we were that day, tucked into the "Fearless Cottage," with him calling me out.

Why was I playing small?

Playing small felt safe and less risky. It felt familiar. The thoughts went something like this, "If I play small, maybe I won't be as disruptive or risk rejection, maybe there is a way to do this in the food industry, without people knowing, without more ridicule. At that point, I'd been called 'food's Erin Brockovich' but did I want that? Maybe if I play small, I won't be harassed or ridiculed? Maybe if I play small, I won't lose my anonymity, it won't change my relationships, and people won't get mad. . . ." It went on and on. I was hiding under a blanket of excuses, and he'd have none of it.

I remember looking at him that day as he told me that I was the right person to get this message out. There was a mirroring. He was reflecting a higher potential back to me, but it felt so unfamiliar.

I knew I would have to throw out all of the excuses I'd made, the reasons for not doing more, for not playing bigger. I was going to have to process all of the fear I felt about the disruption this was going to create, the uncertainty that it would bring. And I was going to have to figure out how to be braver than I'd ever been in my life. It was going to require change on every level.

I'd have to truly believe that I could figure this out. Did I actually believe I could do this? I am not sure I did at that point. I'd graduated as the top woman in my class from business school. I'd been terrified going into that, too. And thankfully, I'd had incredible ethics, entrepreneur, economic, and finance professors at one of the country's top MBA programs. I'd worked on the equity desk with a team that managed $20 billion in assets, meeting with management teams across industries and sectors. I'd earned a full scholarship to business school and landed an incredible job on a team that managed billions in assets, and yet that voice in my head was telling me to play small. That voice was saying, "Who are you to do this?"

Alex was unwavering. And suddenly, in the middle of one of the hardest stretches of my life, a new, unfamiliar voice was telling me the exact opposite of what everyone else was saying. He was telling me to follow this through, when others were telling me it was unobtainable, and reflecting back to me my highest potential.

Why am I sharing this? Because innovation is not just about the operating model and balance sheet. It is such a personal endeavor, and your belief system and who you surround yourself with matter. If you don't believe in yourself, your business lacks a solid foundation, and it will fail. Success requires conviction.

It takes so much courage to step into that role, that ambition, to risk ridicule, rather than to stay small and in the shadows. I understand it, because I had to find the courage too. Sometimes the bravest moments are the ones that no on sees, the quiet moments when you decide that more is possible. Like countless entrepreneurs before, I had to step out of the shadows, holding not only fear, but also ambition, passion, and tenacity, and move forward. And in that friendship with Alex, there was a steadying force, and the realization that I wouldn't have to do it alone.

Find the Ones Who Mirror Your Potential

I remember that meeting so clearly; it was as if Alex were holding a mirror up to me, saying, "See? This is what I see. How can you not see it?" And in all that he was, he was reflecting back to me all that I was. And he made me see it. The parts that I didn't want people to see, the parts that I'd tucked away to try to play small.

Maggie Smith describes it perfectly in her book, *You Can Make This Place Beautiful*, "I made myself small, folded myself up origami tight." That is exactly what I'd done. But it wasn't going to cut it moving forward, and it clearly wasn't cutting it with Alex.

Alex had no tolerance for any of the excuses. He saw the potential.

It changed everything.

I've thought about that day so many different times over the years and why I actually responded to it. It would have been so easy at that point to say, "I wrote the book on our broken food system, that's enough." But the truth is that it was just the starting point. I knew that I could do more, despite all of the haters and naysayers. I knew what I was capable of and that I had only just scratched the surface. He knew it too, and he wanted me to play big.

I've thought about how what he did is one of the greatest things that you can do for a friend, a colleague, or a loved one—reflect back to them all that they are capable of, believe in them so completely that they begin to believe in themselves.

It doesn't matter if you do this for a child, a friend, a colleague, or a loved one. It's one of the greatest gifts you can give someone. It's why I now mentor and coach; it's why I serve on boards and serve in that role for others. It has been my objective ever since: to give that gift to others, to reflect back to them their highest potential, to be a mirror, a light, to help them get out of their own way. To serve as that belief system, that support, that scaffolding. I believe it is one of the greatest gifts that you can give someone, to amplify their fullest potential, so that they can see it themselves and live their fullest life. It's what I hope to do for you, as you read this book, to help you discover and embrace your potential.

Johann Wolfgang von Goethe (1749–1832) is quoted as saying, "At the moment of commitment the entire universe conspires to assist you." That quote comes again in different forms.

Ralph Waldo Emerson said, "Once you make a decision, the universe conspires to make it happen."

And what began to unfold from that moment on changed my life. It was the decision to stop playing small that changed everything. It turned a no to a yes, a roadblock into a detour, and an acceptance began to take shape that I could figure it out. My first book led to a TEDx talk, a speech on our failing food system. That TEDx talk was curated by a woman who leads an organization called "Play Big." My speech has now been translated into dozens of languages and viewed millions of times. It led to consulting and strategy work, with the world's largest food companies reaching out and saying things like, "You can say things we can't say." It led to helping Nestlé formulate their very first allergen-free, organic chocolate chip morsels. It led to global food executives reaching out and sharing their stories about loved ones they'd lost to cancer, loved ones diagnosed with autism, and experiences they'd had working overseas. It led to standing before members of Congress, lobbying for transparency and food labels. It led to launching a financial services firm to help transition food supply chains of companies that are switching to climate-smart agricultural practices. It led to keynotes to the World Bank and global food and finance companies, to what is now this book. Why? Because courage is contagious. Helping someone get out of their own way is one of the greatest gifts you can give them. When one person is brave in their life, it inspires others to do the same.

So it will come as no surprise that I sat down with Alex before I began writing this book.

Unshackling Your Courage

As we put our heads together, and Alex shared his thoughts on fear, leadership, business success, consciousness, and so much more, I relayed some of the thoughts I had that day back in 2010, when he so candidly called me out. I shared with him how shackling some beliefs and relationships had been, almost like chains holding me down. He laughed and said, "You know, in order to live the life you are meant to live, you can't be chained down and play small. Look at the word. You have to lose the 's+m' to get to "all." You can't miss that double meaning because it is so incredibly profound. You have to lose the chains that shackle you, that limit your courage and creativity, in order to be all that you can be. We have to lose the limiting beliefs; the restrictive relationships and mindsets that bind us; the fear that shackles us; the behaviors, beliefs, and patterns that hold us back. You really do have to lose the chains to become *all* that you are meant to be. And for most of us, that may not be an easy task, especially in a culture that values conformity.

I always find it fascinating when another culture or language has a word that we don't have in English. There is an ancient Hindi word that expresses the shackling mindset of "smallness" so beautifully. It is "genshai," and it means to never treat another person in a matter that would make them feel small, including yourself.

There are mental, physical, psychological, and emotional bonds that can hold back the best of us. We see the world as we see ourselves. And we can be our own worst critics. These self-limiting beliefs prevent us from living our purpose, our highest calling. And they may be so familiar that you don't even realize they are there.

Some constraints are self-imposed, and far too many are imposed by society. Freeing ourselves from those constraints requires fortitude and friendship. It requires resources and mentors. It requires humility in acknowledging where our own behaviors and beliefs hold us back. It requires acknowledging our own blind spots to everything from our thought patterns to the systemic discrimination that restricts entire demographics. It requires courage to go into all of that, and fear almost always precedes courage.

Fear is an emotion that controls us from the shadows. It's the parts of us we want no one to see and one of the greatest and heaviest chains that bind us. It can govern so much, sometimes consciously, often subconsciously.

Fear is the ultimate shackle.

And as Alex and I talked about how our subconscious mind is so powerful, he shared: "When I was young, I was afraid. As I got older I learned that fear could be a motivator. I knew myself well enough to work with myself to get by. In my professional life, I was known for being fearless, but I was not. I knew I had to keep all the fear in place, as fear of failure, and away from the creativity where fear would ruin the creativity."

He continued, "The fear I had that was 'subconscious' I could not work with. We can only work with what is conscious, and spiritual work is to make more and eventually all of the mind conscious. For example, I used to say, 'fear is the enemy of creativity,' but now I realize it's not so much the enemy as the opposite of creativity, as an aspect of creation (love). I didn't know the source of fear in the same way I didn't know the source of myself. And all this can be made quite handy in the material world of achievements and egoic hopes to prove that the self can overcome and defeat the world."

He went on, "Business can be a great personal teacher, but it has a huge flaw built into the teaching. Its judgment of success is the accumulation of money and power. This flaw means that it has a ceiling as a spiritual endeavor . . . but deep inquiry can bring forth more loving forms of business."

It is such brave work to do that deep inquiry. It can challenge so much—so many relationships, so many belief systems, and so much of our social conditioning. Thankfully, this deep inner work is becoming more common, and business is expanding beyond its traditional confines, as it diversifies. With transparency and data come an awareness of justice, social responsibility, equity, governance, and ethics. These terms are no longer just buzzwords but values to be explored and integrated. Business is changing.

Coach Lasso's Lesson

Deep inquiry requires curiosity, and curiosity requires courage because knowledge humbles you. And while many now know this quote thanks to Ted Lasso, it was the poet, Walt Whitman, who wrote, "Be curious, not judgmental." With so much new information coming at us so quickly, embracing curiosity is a superpower.

Having an open mind is one of the most important characteristics of any leader. It invites change and expands what's possible, but as we begin learning new things, shame can inevitably creep in when we realize how old behaviors and beliefs no longer serve us.

So what do we fear? Shame is right up there. And as we begin to understand the external costs of past business practices, the destruction and the damage, the dehumanization that has occurred, addressing shame becomes part of the journey.

According to *Scientific American* (Kämmerer, 2019), "We feel shame when we violate the social norms we believe in. At such moments we feel humiliated, exposed, and small and are unable to look another person straight in the eye. We want to sink into the ground and disappear. Shame makes us direct our focus inward and view our entire self in a negative light. Women are quicker to feel humiliated than men, and adolescents feel shame more intensely than adults do." And entrepreneurship in a lot of ways invites shame, as we unlearn and relearn, through its challenges and constant tests. Innovation at its core is violating the status quo and social norm. Just ask the founders of Netflix how they felt when they were shamed out of the room by the Blockbuster team or anyone shamed by an investor or colleague.

According to Carol Kopp (2023), Joseph Schumpeter characterizes creative destruction as "innovations in the manufacturing process that increase productivity," describing it as the "process of industrial mutation that incessantly revolutionizes the economic structure from within, incessantly destroying the old one, incessantly creating a new one." It's an insurgency. Entrepreneurs are violating social norms, challenging the status quo, expectations, and existing realities. When ridicule, naysayers and derision show up, shame and fear can ride shotgun to all of it.

According to Shanelle Mullin (2023), "From an evolutionary perspective, it makes sense that familiarity leads to comfort. Something you're familiar with is less likely to hurt you. Or, at least, hurt you in an unexpected way." So in trying to control for fallout, for fear, for rejection or any shame that may occur in business, we all too often play small.

It gives us a sense of control.

And as I sat with all of this, the courage it takes to understand ourselves, our deepest fears, where they originate from and how to learn to consciously give voice to the subconscious, it's clear that courage is critical to innovation and creativity. The subconscious can dictate what we tolerate, what we accept, who we surround ourselves with, what we do, because it seeks the familiar, and challenging all of that is brave. Even if the familiar abuses us, like business as we know it, the familiarity provides a comfort because it's not abusing us in an unexpected way. So it is brave work to stand up to abuse and the shame that accompanies it. But shame can't coexist with acceptance. Acceptance disinfects shame.

So if the familiar metrics in business are money and power, is there a way to integrate environmental stewardship, equity, diversity, and justice into that formula that drives shareholder value? Absolutely. We now have the data to prove it, and the ultimate power will be in the hands of the businesses who successfully integrate these principles.

It will require a deep understanding of what is happening in the market right now, an examination of both the resources we've taken for granted like clean air and water, and also an examination of long-held beliefs, blind spots, and biases. And that is brave work.

As I have moved through this work, I have excavated things about the food, artificial intelligence, technology, and finance systems at the same time I excavated my own belief system. Beliefs that I'd held my entire life changed, what I tolerated changed, and my support system changed. I learned things for the first time that some had known for generations, and there were moments, months, during this time, where the new knowledge required deep humility.

Action Item: Fear Inventory

Before you go any further, I am going to ask you to do an exercise. Think of it like a "Fear Inventory" to help unload some of the internal dialogue and beliefs that may be holding you down.

Ask yourself: What is holding me back? Is it resources? Time? Money? People? What am I afraid of? What am I ashamed of? What is my deepest fear? Did someone shame me as a child? As an adult? Does that voice still echo in my head? Can I share it with someone? Let it out? Write it down?

Go into those emotions, into those memories—they've held you back for long enough—and bring them to the surface. I've found it's really hard for fear to survive in the light when shared with someone you love. We've all had something terrible happen to us. Visualize, if you can, taking that younger version of yourself, putting an arm around your shoulder, and letting that younger version of you know that you've got support now. Support yourself the same way you'd support your own child, or best friend, or someone you love.

Love disintegrates shame and wraps its arms around fear.

Take a minute to think about these things, to jot them down. No one needs to see them. Simply write them at the end of this chapter or in your Notes app. This exercise will help excavate them and the emotions tied to them. You can shred it, burn it, delete it, or flush the list down the toilet when you're done. Or you can share it with someone you love and trust.

Why am I asking you to do this?

Because the entrepreneurial journey will trigger your deepest insecurities and fears, from presentations to investor meetings, to product launches and product failures. There will be moments of bliss you cannot yet fathom, and there will be moments of grief and anger that will flood you. You will experience the full spectrum of human emotions on this journey.

In order to live your purpose through innovation, to live your most vibrant, fulfilling life, you can't be chained by fear or shame.

You first have to acknowledge what is holding you back. And chances are, you've carried those fears, beliefs, and insecurities around for long enough. It's time to break those chains and stop playing small.

The world needs your unique talents, skillsets, and ideas. No one else in the world has your story, ideas, and experiences. And in a world of conformity and sameness, only you can bring all of that magic to life.

Resources

Kämmerer, A. (2019). The scientific underpinnings and impacts of shame. *Scientific American* [online]. Available at: https://www.scientificamerican .com/article/the-scientific-underpinnings-and-impacts-of-shame/

Knowles, M. (2023). *Belief is truly the first step to achieving anything. When I started* . . . [online]. LinkedIn. Available at: https://www.linkedin .com/posts/mathewknowles_belief-is-truly-the-first-step-to-achieving-activity-7097013679207976960-pWEQ/?utm_source=share&utm _medium=member_ios

Kopp, C. M. (2023). *Creative destruction definition* [online]. Investopedia. Available at: https://www.investopedia.com/terms/c/creativedestruction .asp#:~:text=Schumpeter%20characterized%20creative %20destruction%20as,incessantly%20creating%20a%20new %20one.%22

Mullin, S. (2023, January 19). The science of familiarity: Increasing conversions by being unoriginal. *CXL.* [online]. Available at: https://cxl.com/ blog/science-of-familiarity/#:~:text=From%20an%20evolutionary%20 perspective%2C%20it,want%20to%20risk%20the%20unfamiliar

3

The Eye-popping Return
on Authenticity

*"Weirdness is what sets us apart, gets us hired. Be your unapologetically
weird self. In fact, being weird may even find you the ultimate happiness."*
—Chris Sacca, venture investor, company advisor,
entrepreneur, and lawyer

AFTER AN INCREDIBLE career in advertising, in which he was named
Ad Director of the Decade and won countless awards, my friend Alex
Bogusky stepped down from the advertising agency with his name
on it and founded a private equity firm called Batshit Crazy Ventures.

One of the investments Batshit Crazy made was into a company
called "Liquid Death."

Disruption Takes Courage

Liquid Death is the story of how one guy went "Searching for
Meaning in a Nihilist Can of Water" (Lee, 2023). The company has

a $700 million valuation with $130 million in annual sales, as I write this, after only three years, with the motto, "Murder Your Thirst." According to Lee, the company turned online comments from its biggest haters into a series of music albums. Liquid Death partnered with Martha Stewart to make a $58 candle in the shape of a severed hand. It made and sold a $182 limited edition enema kit (yes, an enema) in partnership with Blink-182 drummer, Travis Barker. In other words, the company's marketing, by any measure, was batshit crazy, and it got the attention of retailers, consumers, and investors.

"If you don't want to drink (alcohol), this is way more fun," cofounder and CEO Mike Cessario told Bloomberg (Lee, 2023) after they secured $70 million in a funding round. The company touts environmental friendliness by using cans, which are more recyclable than plastic bottles, and it aims to get more people to drink water by putting it in a can that resembles the beers our dads drank when we were kids, rather than the island, yoga vibe that the plastic water bottles give off.

If you've ever bought it at a drugstore or gas station, Cessario writes, most likely the person behind the counter has done a double take and laughed that they were about to card you and ask for your ID.

This exact thing happened to me on a recent road trip.

The Liquid Death team took a totally stale category and revolutionized it with their "batshit crazy" investors. While the bottled water industry conformed to the homogeneity of plastic water bottles and polluting the planet, Liquid Death stepped in like a hydration hit squad and captured massive market share with their cans.

So why did this work? Liquid Death wasn't trying to be "the Dasani of Sustainability." They weren't trying to be "the Patagonia of Water Bottles." Cessario wasn't trying to replicate anything that was familiar.

His attitude: this entire category is stale and needs disruption, and he brought his values to it. Instead of cheap plastics that end up in the ocean, he switched to cans. Instead of a yoga vibe, he designed a can for someone hanging out at a party. He made hydration fun.

According to Jim Andrews (2023), "Whether you consider Liquid Death a stunt marketer, shock marketer or anti-marketer, the self-described 'funny beverage company who hates corporate marketing as much as you do' is marketing driven."

Liquid Death first ventured into the space in late 2021 through a promotional partnership with Tony Hawk that offered limited-edition, $500 signature skateboards decorated with paint that had been infused with the legendary skater's blood. Ten percent of the proceeds were donated to anti-plastic nonprofit 5 Gyres and Hawk's The Skatepark Project.

In 2022, Liquid Death entered professional and college sports, according to Andrews, "by staging a combine for NFL and collegiate 'hydration assistants' that in addition to reminding us not to call them water boys, selected a winner—Travis Paulson of the Indianapolis Colts—to receive a $100,000 endorsement deal and his own ad."

The company has also released campaigns with Jalen Green, the NBA guard for the Houston Rockets, who is also an investor, showcasing a retro-themed horror-comedy commercial playing a pick-up game with a severed head. Along with the 60-second spot, the company sold a $125 Hoop Head collectible basketball on its website.

Your First Ingredient Is Capital

Liquid Death isn't trying to please everyone, and its investors give the company latitude for creativity in its marketing. Which brings me to an important point: the capital you partner with is the first ingredient that goes into your product. Choose wisely because the values that govern your capital will govern your company. As you enter into a partnership with your investors, it's important to consider how creative, risk averse, courageous, and diverse your investors are. Does your cap table have blind spots? In other words, do your investors serve as informed advisors and guides? One of the most important ingredients in any product is the capital, which we will get into in more detail in Chapter 9.

Cessario recently shared, "A great piece of advice my dad gave me a long time ago: Don't confuse effort with results. Anyone can dig a deep hole, but few can find buried treasure."

He goes on, "In this current state of 'hustle' mentality, there may be too much value placed on working hard, grinding, total dedication, etc. But hard work is a waste of time if you're doing the wrong thing or if your idea sucks. We need less emphasis on 'hustle' and more emphasis on self-awareness and being okay with not being right—and instead having the skill set on how to *find* right. Because nine times out of ten, the right thing isn't obvious and rarely what you predict it will be."

The right thing isn't always obvious, and it certainly isn't always easiest. You can hustle and grind and blow through millions of dollars with nothing to show for it. So how do you figure it out?

The Liquid Death team looked at the data on plastics and created an entirely different experience for the consumer, disrupting a stale and homogenous category. To them and countless customers, plastic water bottles are intolerable, as intolerable as going to a Blockbuster store to rent a movie when you know there is a smarter option. And it turns out, plastic waste and plastic pollution are intolerable to a growing number of asset managers and investors too. They don't want the liability. They want to bet on companies that are good for people and the planet. Why? Because the number of lawsuits taking aim at companies that are polluting the planet are growing. Externalized costs are being recognized for the liability they are. As I wrote this, in a moment of complete serendipity, a lawsuit was filed against Pepsi for externalizing the costs of their plastic water bottles in the form of plastic pollution (Khan, 2023).

Which brings me to another incredible model that decided to look at beverage data differently, a team that creatively disrupted beer category.

NoLo's Superpower

According to a Gallup poll conducted in 2021 (Brenan, 2021), 40% of U.S adults say they do not consume alcoholic beverages, such as liquor, wine, or beer—among the lowest marks recorded during the last two decades—up from 35% in 2019.

You'd never know that 40% of U.S. adults say they don't consume alcohol, given how pervasive and enormous the advertising by the alcohol industry is (Jernigan, 2008).

Alcohol companies spend about $2 billion a year on advertising in the United States alone, according to Jernigan (2008). But despite that spending, alcohol consumption patterns are changing (Sabetta, 2023).

Global sales of no- and low-alcohol category (now called "NoLo") topped $11 billion in 2022, with growth expected to accelerate in the coming years (Aswani, 2022). The data firm ISWR said consumer demand for no- and low-alcohol products rose more than 7% in volume across 10 key global markets in 2022. The category is forecast to post a compound annual growth rate topping 7% through 2026—double digits in the United States. Friends in the private equity world are taking notice too, as these "NoLo" options continue to multiply at industry trade shows.

Liquid Death caught that wave with an authenticity that is uniquely theirs, and so did a brand called Athletic Brewing Company.

"With shoppers, especially younger-aged groups showing a willingness to go between alcohol and products that contain a little or none of it, brands such as Guinness, Heineken, Corona, and Budweiser have offerings that straddle both categories," according to Christopher Doering (2023).

The growth has attracted the attention of companies that traditionally haven't played in the space. In November 2022, Keurig Dr Pepper purchased a minority stake in Athletic Brewing through a $50 million investment in the nonalcoholic craft beer maker (Doering, 2023). The number should not be lost on you. It's the same number that Netflix offered Blockbuster. Keurig Dr Pepper didn't have paradigm blindness like Blockbuster and has so far avoided Blockbuster's fate.

In a GQ article, Gabriella Paiella (2023) asks, "How, exactly, did Athletic Brewing Company turn one of the most unappealing, underwhelming, and frankly all-time depressing beverages into a booming $60 million a year business? How did it pocket a $50 million investment from Keurig Dr Pepper, land partnerships with Netflix and JetBlue, and sweep top prizes at beer contests around the globe? How did it build a loyal customer base, 80% of which drinks alcohol but still chooses to pay almost $15 for a six-pack for the nonalcoholic stuff? Beyond that, how did it become an inescapable modern brand, one that has—can by can—changed the way we drink?"

According to cofounder Bill Shufelt, "It turns out over 30% of people [in America] don't drink at all, and almost 60% of people barely drink. That's a ton of money left on the table, so the economic opportunity was obvious to me. Everyone always thought the occasion base for nonalcoholic beer was one percent of one percent of the time. It's pretty much totally the opposite—*most people are not drinking most of the time.*"

Flip the Script

So how did the Athletic Brewing team flip the script and figure it all out? Before founding Athletic Beer, Shufelt worked for a hedge fund and was into endurance racing. According to Paiella (2023), "He was a work hard, play hard kind of guy, and both included a lot of socializing over alcohol. To feel and perform better, he decided to take a break from alcohol."

At the suggestion of his wife, he quit his job to found his own nonalcoholic brewery. Getting a brewer to partner with him—now, that was the tough part. Shufelt endured dozens of rejections before he met John Walker. The craft brewer had been making a living for the past 15 years in New Mexico but was looking to move his family back to his home state.

According to Paiella (2023), "What makes Athletic taste so mind-bogglingly similar to *beer* is the brewing process. Most nonalcoholic beer is regular beer, usually a macro lager, that has the ethanol boiled off at the end. An afterthought, a subtraction—and that's exactly what it tastes like."

"Once you start doing that, you change the chemistry. You change the mouthfeel and you change the experience," Walker says.

Walker, meanwhile, wondered: What if you just added things together to result in a nonalcoholic craft beer, instead of an alcoholic beer that needed to be altered? He developed a proprietary and secret process to do just that. "We're able to design recipes exactly as they should be and respect the ingredients," he says.

Today, Athletic Brewing is the number two nonalcoholic beer in the country, but it is on track to surpass Heineken 0.0. And while beer sales in general are plummeting, the nonalcoholic category is growing. At the time when Athletic Brewing launched, non-alcoholic beer made up 0.3% of beer sales; now it's closer to 2%. According to Nielsen, the American nonalcoholic beer market was worth $328.6 million in 2022, 19.5% more than it was in 2021 (Paiella, 2023).

How to Trend Spot

I've been early to spot trends. Data always tell a story. I learned this early on in my investment career, during my days at the equity desk, and it's served me well ever since. Today, I'd be called a futurist. My cofounders at rePlant called me a "market maker." Data tell a story, and it's a smart way to future-proof your business. One of the earliest examples of this in my career was when I was invited to meet with Nestlé, shortly after my first TEDx talk went online. The CEO of its frozen food division reached out and said, "You can say things I can't say. I'd like to invite you in to speak with our team."

When I sat down with his team in Solon, Ohio, the company was losing market share, sales were down, and morale was in the tank. I asked them if they were proud of what they were selling. Not a single hand went up. How can you expect anyone to drive revenue and sales if they don't believe in what they are doing? We got to work examining the market shifts and the opportunities to engage with a twenty-first century consumer. I asked them, as I do all of my clients, "Where can you be braver in your work?"

Seven years later, I got the answer. An email came through one morning from Nestlé, "Robyn, we did it! We met your challenge and launched the company's first organic, allergen-free chocolate chip morsel!" Change doesn't happen overnight. Recreating these systems that we've inherited takes time. But trend spotting, leveraging data, is a powerful skillset. It opens up market opportunities and new demographics. And the team at Athletic Brewing has it. They saw something others didn't.

"Seventy-five percent of nonalcoholic beer drinkers were over age 45 when we started," Shufelt says. "That has flipped. Seventy-five percent are under age 45 now."

In other words, the drinking paradigm and rules for one generation are different to the rules, behaviors, and paradigms of another. This is hardly surprising. It is the same for music, fashion, media, technology, and other industries.

According to Claura Ludmir (2023),

> One of the macro trends that has grown over the past few years and is intrinsically linked to the boom of health and wellness is mindful drinking and the "NoLo" movement, with millennials and Gen Z driving the demand for alternatives to alcoholic beverages.
>
> The nonalcoholic category is expanding thanks to both higher demand and innovation within the space, with volumes expected to grow by 25% between 2022 and 2026. The world's largest brewer, Anheuser-Busch InBev, aims for its no- and low-alcohol beers to account for one fifth of sales by 2025.
>
> Why? Gen Z drinks, on average, 20% less than millennials, who also drink less than the previous generation, mainly because of an increased awareness of the dangers and effects of alcohol and the rise of health-consciousness as a lifestyle. In fact, an overwhelming 86% of Gen Z consumers believe that their mental health is as significant as their physical health when considering drinking alcohol.

JetBlue recently became the first airline in the United States serving nonalcoholic beer following a partnership with Athletic Brewing Company.

So why did Athletic Brewing work, amidst a sea of naysayers and sameness? An unapologetic obsession on figuring out how to rethink nonalcoholic beer, one with its own unique formulation process and design. Instead of accepting the status quo and leaning into the same brewing process as alcoholic beer and simply subtracting an ingredient at the end, the team reinvented the entire design process. They leveraged their unique skills and experience and built a brand that was entirely their own. Just like the team at Liquid Death.

According to Paiella (2023),

What all the wellness and biohacking bros seem to miss is something else that's crucial to our health. Maybe even the most crucial of all: community. Take the Blue Zones, the regions on earth that have been identified as where people live the longest. Along with eating whole food diets and staying active, what sets these places apart is a tight-knit sense of community.

And that might be the single most appealing thing that Athletic has provided people. We're already in an existing nationwide loneliness epidemic. If you're not drinking alcohol, for whatever reason—from sobriety to marathon training—it can add to the sense of isolation.

Even if chugging beer isn't physically healthy, there's something about cracking open a cold one around other people that is. Athletic proved that it doesn't have to be alcoholic to provide the same much-needed ritual pleasure.

The growth in "NoLo" beverages that are free from alcohol parallels the growth seen in "better for you," "free from" food, with consumers seeking better for you options. It's not going away, as a growing number of health conditions impact our families. As a matter of fact, it's only getting stronger, as consumers learn more about how products are not only impacting their health but also the health of the planet. As I write this, "NoLo" is one of the fastest growing categories in food and beverages.

Eco-anxious Institutional Investors

There is a new term for the worry that is created in a generation growing up with headlines about the environment and climate change: eco-anxiety. And the younger consumers want to know that your brand is doing everything it can to be part of the solution and not part of the problem.

And plastic water bottles? They are definitely part of the problem. According to the United Nations, "Our planet is choking on plastic." The UN reports (n.d.), "We have become addicted to single-use plastic products—with severe environmental, social, economic, and health consequences." In a lot of ways, plastic is the new tobacco. Only it's not just bad for us, but also the planet.

Why does this matter? According to Fidelity International (2023): "It is estimated that more than 50% of global GDP is moderately or highly dependent on nature. The 'Global Risks Report 2023' by the World Economic Forum has ranked 'biodiversity loss' among the top five 'risks that may have the most severe impact over the next ten years.'"

Investors aren't messing around.

Fidelity International goes on to say, "While climate change is undoubtedly one of the most significant risks to the long-term profitability and sustainability of companies, biodiversity loss is an equally pressing issue that investors cannot ignore."

And how exactly do they define biodiversity?

According to the Fidelity Investment report, "Biodiversity loss refers to the gradual reduction in the variety and abundance of life on Earth. Biodiversity loss is driven by five key factors: land and sea use change, pollution, overexploitation, climate change, and invasive species. Biodiversity refers to the living component of natural capital, which more broadly encompasses the world's stock of natural resources, including geology (rocks and minerals), soil, air, and water."

But here's the thing: in business, we don't put biodiversity, soil, water, clean air, and natural capital on the balance sheet. Even though Fidelity is telling us straight up that business is at risk because we keep degenerating these resources. When you put things like clean air, clear water, and bees together, they "provide ecosystem services, such as pollination and food production, air circulation, climate regulation, flood protection, and carbon sequestration, from which we derive social, economic and cultural benefits." And again, "ecosystem" isn't on any balance sheet, but every company depends on it.

See the problem here? Investors are taking notice.

If you've got a product that is *not* destroying the planet, investors are paying attention. It mitigates risk; it makes your company more marketable, with a longer term value proposition. Companies like Liquid Death aren't just trying to murder thirst but also the competition that is wreaking environmental havoc.

According to the United Nations, again, hardly a wild-eyed, activist organization, "Around the world, one million plastic bottles are purchased every minute, while up to five trillion plastic bags are used worldwide every year. In total, half of all plastic produced is designed for single-use purposes—used just once and then thrown away."

Was it always like this? Not at all. According to the UN, from the 1950s to the 1970s, only a small amount of plastic was produced, and the waste it produced was pretty manageable. But then between the 1970s and the 1990s, plastic waste generation more than tripled, as production increased. And then in the early 2000s, according to the UN, the amount of plastic waste we generated rose more in a single decade than it had in the previous 40 years. And today? We produce about 400 million tons of plastic waste every year.

In one generation, plastic pollution exploded. According to the UN, "We are seeing other worrying trends. Since the 1970s, the rate of plastic production has grown faster than that of any other material. If historic growth trends continue, global production of primary plastic is forecasted to reach 1,100 million tonnes by 2050." Eighty-five percent of which ends up in landfills or as unregulated waste. I can't even begin to wrap my head around that number and why it's allowed, given what we already know about biodiversity loss. Apparently, investors feel the same way.

The UN Environment Program (n.d.) is not kidding when it wrote, "Our planet is choking on plastic." Of the seven billion tons of plastic waste generated globally so far, less than 10% has been recycled. Millions of tons of plastic waste are lost to the environment, or sometimes shipped thousands of kilometers to destinations where it is mostly burned or dumped. The estimated annual loss in the value of plastic packaging waste during sorting and processing alone is US$80–120 billion.

So is it any wonder that a company like Liquid Death is attracting investors? It's not a batshit crazy idea; it's a brilliant one. And what is crazy is that the plastic water bottle companies are allowed to keep polluting the planet. So keep an eye on that water cooler, because the markets move faster than policy makers.

But governments are key actors here too. They can eliminate the plastic products we do not need, through bans, for example. They can also promote innovation so the plastics we use are designed and brought to market in a way that allows for their reuse.

And the industry? It can be more transparent so consumers can make informed purchases. They can also increase the use of recycled content in new products in order to upcycle and repurpose or abandon plastics and use cans.

And individuals? There is a lot that we can do—from getting involved with policy, running for office like my friend Laurie, asking the restaurants that you frequent to stop using plastic straws and utensils, bringing your own coffee mug and water bottle to work, bringing your own bags to the grocery store, and pressuring your local authorities to improve how they manage your city's plastic waste. We all play a role.

And just as the early years of the free-from movement had plenty of naysayers and nonbelievers, the same exists here. There will be those who claim this is just a trend, a health and wellness fad that will pass. Don't count on it. Once consumers learn about a product and its impact on their health, they don't unlearn it. And where it may be tempting to marginalize or dismiss these early adopters, you do so at your own risk. Plastic water bottles aren't suddenly going to stop polluting the planet. Younger generations aren't suddenly going to stop caring about what is happening to the planet. Industry-funded science may continue to refute the extent of the damage, but the plastic waste problem isn't going away, and the environmental impact is growing.

The ultimate success of Liquid Death just may be when the entire water cooler at the gas station is full of cans, not just theirs, but their competitors too. Liquid Death isn't just a product, it's an influencer, just like Athletic Brewing.

Land Investors Using Your Secret Sauce

The success of Liquid Death and Athletic Brewing show exactly how consumers are taking their health and the health of the planet into their own hands, quite literally, and what they choose to drink is a powerful way to do that. Smart investors are paying attention.

So stay focused. There will always be noise and naysayers. I cannot emphasize enough how important it is to not get distracted by your competition or what others tell you that you *should* be doing. Lean into your purpose, your why, and lean into the data. Build your supportive scaffolding so that you don't dilute your own secret sauce.

Liquid Death and Athletic Brewing very much each have their own secret sauce. They know their strengths, they know what they are capable of doing, and they've found partners and investors who believe in the vision too.

Plenty of experts will tell you that you need to change your formula, do something one of the successful brands is doing to be able to attain success. Stay true to your vision, ask for help, ask for introductions, but don't compromise who you are, because you are the one to bring this concept to life, given your unique skills, experience, and insight.

As you get to work, you'll want to make sure that you have a few things covered and develop material that investors will request. They include but are not limited to the following:

Business Plan: This will detail your vision, the business opportunity, competitive landscape, and even testimonials and any proof of concept or traction you may already have in the marketplace. Be clear, straightforward, and respectful of the time of the person reading your business plan. Get to the point.

Financial Projections: You will need to forecast your potential profits and losses, revenues and other financial metrics. You can easily get tied up here, because you are providing information based on future projections. Do your homework and research so that you can back up what you state. Also know that no matter what happens, you most likely will have to change these projections, as market conditions change and you build out your team and operating model. Make sure to set realistic assumptions that you can defend.

Team: Investors will want to know who is behind the vision and plan. They will want to know the backgrounds, the experience, the networks, passions, worth ethics, and personalities of the team, and what makes you as the founder an investable asset. They will want to know that when they put money into the business concept that you can steward this successfully, tap your network for help, and they will assess the capabilities and experience of your team to your ability to execute the business plan successfully.

Legal and Compliance Requirements: Hire the best attorney you can afford, and if possible, lean into your network for legal referrals. Ask for recommendations from those who have already been through the startup experience. You will want to have an understanding of compliance requirements which may include incorporation, fund structure, trademarks, intellectual property protection, and regulatory requirements.

Due Diligence Materials: Investors may request additional documentation during their due diligence process, including financial statements, legal contracts, and market analysis reports. You may also want to include market research, testimonials, partnership contracts and any other supporting documents that provide proof of concept.

Before reaching out to an investor, research and understand their specific needs, understand their focus, their investment thesis, so that you deliver the most compelling material to them and for them for their review.

And lastly, rather than send the material as attachments, deliver the material through a file sharing site and pitch deck hosting platforms that enable you to share easily, to track data and information (like how much time is spent in the document, which pages receive the most views, etc.). Using these platforms makes it easy to share links and material with your investor. Dropbox, Google Drive, and Pitch XO are a few common ones that are easy to use and access, and you will be able to capture valuable data about how investors are interfacing with your documents.

A Successful Cover-Up

Which brings me to the wisdom of Jamie Kern Lima. In 2008, Kern Lima cofounded IT Cosmetics after having problems with makeup products due to rosacea and hyperpigmentation. The business struggled for years as beauty retailers rejected her products. Kern Lima was featured on a 10-minute QVC segment in which she wiped her makeup off, revealing her bare face to illustrate the use of IT Cosmetics concealers. All products sold out by the end of the segment.

By 2015, the company had more than $182 million in net sales. She appeared in more than 1,000 live QVC shows, where IT Cosmetics became the largest beauty brand on QVC's network. IT Cosmetics was acquired by L'Oréal for $1.2 billion in 2016. Kern Lima then went on to become L'Oréal's first female CEO. She also was the first person in her family to attend college.

Kern Lima shared on Instagram,

In a world that glorifies conformity and sameness, it can be hard to stay true to your own unique ideas and vision. You may have a new idea or a different perspective that's exciting and fresh, but that may be met with skepticism, criticism, or disapproval from others. You may be told that it's too risky, too weird, or too radical, and that you should just stick to the tried-and-true formulas that others have already used.

There are so many people in the early years of my work who said this. But if you conform to others' fears, others' expectations, the status quo, you may avoid rejection, ridicule and criticism, but you will miss out on the fullest expression of your creativity.

Staying small won't serve the world. Like Kern Lima experienced, there will be many in your world who will want you to stay small, who won't understand your vision.

This is where the entrepreneurial journey may start to get hard. Where your commitment may be challenged by relationships, by social conditioning, and the pressure to conform. It is where strength and tenacity start to kick in. Where you will need to make sure that the people you've got around you are unwavering, honest, and committed to seeing you succeed; otherwise, that fear of rejection and criticism will throw you way off course. You will need your allies who have your back, who want you to succeed. And you will need to know and remember, deep down, what you are made of.

Because as you grow into your leadership role, you will need to *do you*, unapologetically and authentically you. Your authenticity cannot be duplicated.

Know Your Strengths

This reminds me of a story from early in my career. I was in New York for a food industry conference. My team sent me to the New York Stock Exchange to meet some of our traders. It was late November and extremely cold out. When I got there, the guys asked if I wanted to run a trade. This was before we'd digitized and automated everything, and they handed me a slip of paper and pointed me in the direction that I needed to go. On the count of three, they told me to run. I threw off my winter coat and ran a trade across the floor of the New York Stock Exchange.

When I got back to them, their mouths were hanging open. What my winter coat had hidden was that I was six months pregnant. They began apologizing profusely, which I stopped immediately. I said, "If I wasn't comfortable doing it, I'd have told you." So at six months pregnant, I ran a trade across the floor of the New York Stock Exchange in heels.

Why am I telling you this? Know your strengths and skills, believe in what you can do, prove it to yourself and to others. And if you need help, ask for it. Don't let others' opinions or beliefs limit you.

Action Steps: Resilience Inventory

I want you to jot down what we are going to call your *resilience inventory*, the things you do to stay strong. What happens when you are down? Who do you call? What do you do? What habits do you have in place to handle rejection that you are proud of? And what habits do you have in place that you probably wish no one knew? And what about how you cope with criticism? Make a list of those go-to items. Again, remember—no shame. Just download the list at the end of this chapter, on your phone or tablet. Call one side Keep. These are the habits you're proud of and want to keep. Call the other Release—the habits you'd prefer to release. Let's keep going.

Resources

Andrews, J. (2023). *Will Liquid Death breathe life into partnerships?* [online]. TicketManager. Available at: https://ticketmanager.com/will-liquid-death-breathe-life-into-partnerships/

Aswani, S. (2022). *No- and low-alcohol category value surpasses $11bn in 2022* [online]. IWSR. Available at: https://www.theiwsr.com/no-and-low-alcohol-category-value-surpasses-11bn-in-2022/

Brenan, M. (2021). *U.S. alcohol consumption on low end of recent readings* [online]. Gallup.com. Available at: https://news.gallup.com/poll/353858/ alcohol-consumption-low-end-recent-readings.aspx?utm_source= alert&utm_medium=email&utm_content=morelink&utm_campaign= syndication

Doering, C. (2022). Keurig Dr Pepper invests $50M in Athletic Brewing. *Food Dive* [online]. Available at: https://www.fooddive.com/news/ keurig-dr-pepper-invests-50m-in-athletic-brewing-nonalcoholic -beer/636125/

Doering, C. (2023). No- and low-alcohol category tops $11B in 2022 with growth accelerating, IWSR says. *Food Dive* [online]. Available at: https://www.fooddive.com/news/no-and-low-alcohol-category-tops- 11b-in-2022-with-growth-accelerating-iw/642648/

Fidelity International. (2023). *Sleeping giant: Bond markets are critical in the fight against biodiversity loss* [online]. Available at: https://s3-eu-west-1 .amazonaws.com/germanfrontdoorv4prod-live-1324fb6294be47ceb 7851ec22521-174be63/Germany%20PI/Pdf%20documents/sleeping- giant-biodiversity.pdf

Jernigan, D. (2008). Intoxicating brands: Alcohol advertising and youth. *Multinational Monitor*, 30(1). Available at: https://www .multinationalmonitor.org/mm2008/072008/jernigan.html#:~:text =Alcohol%20companies%20spend%20close%20to,in%20the%20 United%20States%20alone

Khan, M. (2023). New York sues PepsiCo in effort to hold it responsible for litter that winds up in rivers. *AP News* [online]. Available at: https://apnews.com/article/pepsico-buffalo-river-drinking-water- new-york-59bcaa6bd324bab5c4c683fea2801db0

Lee, M. (2023). *Searching for meaning in a can of nihilist water. Future Market* [online]. Available at: https://thefuturemarket.substack.com/ p/searching-for-meaning-in-a-can-of?utm_source=profile&utm_ medium=reader2

Ludmir, C. (2023). Why GenZ is drinking less and what this means for the alcohol industry. *Forbes* [online]. Available at: https://www.forbes .com/sites/claraludmir/2023/06/27/why-genz-is-drinking-less-and-what- this-means-for-the-alcohol-industry/?sh=6f4708c448d1

Paiella, G. (2023). How Athletic Beer won over America. *GQ* [online]. Available at: https://www.gq.com/story/how-athletic-beer-won-america

Sabetta, L. (2023, May 17). Alcohol brands acting more cautious with ad spends. *Beverage Industry* [online]. Available at: https://www.bevindustry .com/articles/95834-alcohol-brands-acting-more-cautious-with-ad-spends#

UN Environment Programme (n.d.). *Beat plastic pollution* [online]. Available at: https://www.unep.org/interactives/beat-plastic-pollution /?gclid=CjwKCAjwo9unBhBTEiwAipC115p3iTgxdOAzDXsN5lV5 ajgctBuATW2TL0_ldBh10kR6gNatMSGUFBoCCtMQAvD_BwE

4

Venture Capital's Biases

"People don't care how much you know until they know how much you care."

—Cynt Marshall, CEO, Dallas Mavericks

IT TAKES A lot of courage to drive change. It's a character trait that I admire deeply and why I was excited to learn about the work of the Fearless Fund.

According to the Fearless Fund website,

We know that companies with a female founder perform 63% better on average than all-male founding teams (according to First Round Capital, 2015). Despite a greater potential to produce higher returns, women are historically underfunded, particularly women of color.

In 2018, U.S. companies raised a total of $130 billion in venture capital funding, yet only 2.2% of that total went toward female-founded companies and less than % of total funding was allocated toward businesses founded by women of color (Girlboss, 2019). It's only gotten worse.

Fearless Fund was established to address the gap that exists in venture capital funding for women of color (WOC)-led businesses and to finally push the needle on the abysmal statistics that drive the current narrative for WOC-led businesses today.

For someone operating from an outdated paradigm, this may feel like a threat, a challenge to the rules that they know, the rules that worked for them. They're not going to recognize the paradigm blindness and market shifts happening here, and some will push back, which is exactly what is happening to the Fearless Fund as I write this.

According Alexandra Olson (2023), "The Fearless Fund is a tiny player in the approximately $200 billion global venture capital market. The Atlanta-based firm has invested nearly $27 million in some 40 businesses led by women of color since launching in 2019, and awarded another $3.7 million in grants. Collectively, those businesses employ about 540 people, up from 250 at the time of investment, according to the Fearless Fund's 'impact report.'"

"The Fearless Fund is a minnow in the VC world of more than $200 billion in assets, less than 0.05 percent of which goes to startups founded by Black women," wrote Michelle Celarier (2023), and it's being targeted in a lawsuit that is provoking outrage and renewed commitment to diversity, equity, and inclusion (DEI) strategies. If you've ever wondered what it looks like to challenge the status quo, the Fearless Fund is a powerful example.

The Power of the Purse

Today, women control roughly one-third of total household financial assets in the United States. If you have any doubt about this financial fortitude, look to the recent success of the Taylor Swift and Beyonce tours and of the blockbuster success of the *Barbie* movie. *Barbie* smashed box office records and became Warner Brothers' highest grossing film of all time. *Fortune* (Shin, 2023) reported that "Taylor Swift is so important to the economy that she's in the latest Fed report." And according to *Ellevest*, the concerts and movies arguably kept the United States out of recession, as women flexed their economic muscle. U.S. GDP increased $4.3 billion as a result of Taylor Swift's first 53 concerts, with Beyonce's concert tour and movie mirroring equal economic strength. Over the next decade, women are poised to inherit a large share of assets currently held by the baby boomer generation. Moreover, many women will inherit twice—once from their parents and once from their spouses or partners. By 2030, according to Angela Parsons (2023), "Women will hold more than two-thirds of wealth in the United States, setting the stage for women to grow their philanthropic impact."

In his book, *Power vs. Force, The Hidden Determinants of Human Behavior*, David R. Hawkins (2006) examines the source of power:

> Power arises from meaning. It has to do with motive, and it has to do with principle. Power is always associated with that which supports the significance of life itself.
>
> It appeals to that in human nature which we call noble, in contrast to force, which appeals to that which we call crass. Power appeals to that which uplifts, dignifies, ennobles. Force must always be justified, whereas power requires no justification. Force is associated with the partial, power with the whole.

A lot of companies are working to build out their DEI (diversity, equity, inclusion) strategy. So why are some failing and others succeeding? It comes down to power versus force, paradigms, and whether or not you are treating this as a box-ticking exercise, a way for a board to pat itself on the back and award executives bigger bonuses, or a full-scale paradigm shift with integration of DEI into the values of your company. Hint: You want full integration.

Racially diverse founding teams outperform their peers, returning 30% more capital to investors when they reach exit by acquisition or IPO (Ganesan et al., 2023). According to Ganesan et al., "Beyond the larger macroeconomic gains, founders with greater gender and ethnic diversity achieve 30% higher returns for investors upon exit than their white men founder counterparts," and yet racial gaps exist across the U.S. labor market, ultimately manifesting as a $220 billion annual wage disparity across all industries.

Read that again. "Founders with greater gender and ethnic diversity achieve 30% higher returns for investors upon exit than their white men founder counterparts."

Diversity Pays Dividends

If a company's fiduciary duty is to drive shareholder return, and racially diverse founding teams outperform their peers by 30%, then "paradigm blindness" is impacting performance and profitability. We don't understand what we don't yet know.

I am reminded of a conversation I had with a friend who worked for a large food company. The company was trying to figure out how it could boost sales of its granola, especially to Black families. "Black families don't eat a lot of traditional granola products," he shared with management. It was a simple truth, and it was also a blind spot for management because they lacked diversity at senior levels. They were asking the wrong questions, pouring money into the wrong build out. They lacked the knowledge and experience of a company like Soul Grain granola. Soul Grain is where science and art meet. According to the company's website, it is "a female led, minority owned business whose aim is to liven up and diversity the granola industry by exploring the vibrant spices, seasoning and flavors of the Black diaspora and more." How many times has this happened?

A lot. When there is a failure to integrate equity and inclusion into senior leadership decisions and governance, it can backfire. The same holds true for issues of sexual identity and expression.

Alison Taylor, a professor at NYU, wrote on LinkedIn (2023) about the powerful need to embrace diversity, equity and inclusion: "The acceptance of freedom of sexual expression is clear to me in the classroom every day, in fact it seems a particularly dramatic generational shift. Also, this is a human rights issue. There is no neutral middle ground, any more than there was during anti-apartheid or civil rights movements."

Is this vision always accepted at the time? Not at all. Remember Martin Luther King Jr. had a 63% disapproval rating when he was leading the civil rights movement for equity and equality. The same thing is happening here, and hindsight will bring clarity.

So what is a company to do? Consumers aren't one-size-fits-all, and the landscape of DEI is expanding in real time, every day. Just set foot in any classroom, and you will see the changes. Whether you agree with them or not, the changes are happening. And perhaps, that's one of the most important things to understand as a business leader.

On the history and future of corporate boycotts, Daniel Deirmeier predicts a new era of caution saying, "You just have to be clear on what happens. If you say, 'This is so important to me that I think this is core to my values, this is a human-rights issue and I am going to put a stake on the ground'—I have total respect for that. If you waffle, both sides will attack. If you don't know enough to stand your ground, learn."

Diversity of governance will go a long way to mitigating this risk because your team will consist of leaders with varying experiences.

If nature has taught us anything, it's that homogeneous systems fail. Homogenous boards will fail on this changing landscape. They lack the depth and breadth of experience to account for the demographic changes occurring in the marketplace. The telltale sign of someone aging into obsolescence is a closed mind. What was meaningful to one generation is going to change for the next. And right now, the workplace is experiencing seismic shifts, with five generations working side by side. The twenty-first century consumer is demanding more and is going to attach meaning to a brand's action (or inaction).

Diversity of your cap table, governance, and board will mitigate this risk and drive returns. Are you tokenizing the efforts or truly valuing them? Because if you tokenize, you're setting yourself up for a business suicide of sorts.

Finding Meaning

According to Hawkins in *Power vs. Force* (2006), "Meaning is so important that when life loses meaning, suicide commonly ensues. When life loses meaning, we first go into depression; when life becomes less meaningful, we finally leave it. Force has transient goals; when those goals are reached, there remains the emptiness of meaninglessness. Power on the other hand motivates us endlessly. If our lives are dedicated for instance to enhancing the welfare of others and everyone we contact, our lives can never lose meaning. If the purpose of our life, on the other hand, is merely financial success, what happens after that has been attained?"

So how can a company capture more meaning, to ensure its success not only in the short term but also in the long term? What gives a company that purpose, a meaning that ultimately builds consumer loyalty, repeat purchasing, employee retention, and long-term value?

Hawkins wrote, "Love, compassion and forgiveness which may be mistakenly seen by some as submissive are in fact profoundly empowering. Revenge, judgmentalism and condemnation on the other hand inevitably make you go weak. Therefore, regardless of moral righteousness, it is a simple clinical fact that in the long run, the weak cannot prevail against the strong. That which is weak fails of its own accord."

So ask yourself a question that is not usually asked in business: Is your business motivated by love and compassion? It sounds strange, but it's not really. Think back to Yvon Chouinard. He started Patagonia because of his love for the outdoors. Sara Blakely started Spanx because she loved helping women feel better about themselves. Jessica Chastain started Freckle Films because she had compassion for the struggles women had in the film industry with wage discrimination. Reese Witherspoon started a production company called Hello Sunshine that creates projects that center around women's stories. Trevor Rozier-Byrd started Stackwell, an early stage startup on a mission to attack the racial wealth gap by empowering a new community of Black investors—specifically Black millennials and Gen Z. He launched the company in early 2022 after earlier chapters at State Street and other institutions (Knickerbocker, 2023). There was purpose and meaning behind the motivation of each company.

Partake in Changing Markets

Which brings me to my friend, Denise Woodard, the founder of Partake Foods.

Woodard worked at Coca-Cola when her daughter, Vivienne, was born, and like millions of Americans, Woodard's life was disrupted when her daughter developed multiple food allergies. The food allergy demographic is another group that was previously ignored. A lot of early advocacy had to happen, and data continue to support the growth of the sector. Today, the food allergy consumer is taking market share and expanding categories. But it hasn't always been that way and is a great reminder not to dismiss fundamental market movements as "moments."

Created in 2016, Partake Foods exists to offer a selection of delicious, allergy-friendly foods that those with and without food restrictions can enjoy and share with confidence. All offerings are certified gluten-free, non-GMO, vegan, and are free of the top nine allergens (wheat, tree nuts, peanuts, milk, eggs, soy, fish, sesame, and shellfish). Woodard didn't want her daughter to be left out, so she literally created a brand that let her daughter partake in everyday situations where food was often found and celebrated.

She is living the entrepreneurial experience in full transparency, expanding on initiatives, moving through rejection, and not only listening to the marketplace but also responding to basic, human needs.

To get her business, Partake Foods, off the ground, Woodard maxed out her credit cards, emptied her 401(k), and sold her engagement ring. She was met with more than 85 investment rejections before becoming the first Black woman to raise a million dollars in seed capital for a packaged food brand. The resiliency required to do that cannot be underestimated. Woodard faced a lot of challenges raising money in the early stages of Partake Foods. Most investors she met with were men who did not relate to what she was doing nor did they understand the value of her brand. So even with all her years of experience at Coca-Cola, she encountered close to 100 nos from investors.

In a *Marie Claire* article (Klich, 2023), Woodard shared: "My personal identity is tied to the overarching mission of Partake, so I never questioned making the financial decisions I did to be able to grow the business. I felt confident in what I was doing and managed to keep a strong sense of self and positive mental outlook."

By 2020, Woodard raised Series A funding from investors like Rihanna and Marcy Venture Partners (co-founded by Jay-Z); other backers include Grammy Award–winning singer H.E.R., Seattle Seahawks' Bobby Wagner, Black Star Fund, and Once Upon a Farm CEO John Foraker, to name a few. To date, she has raised more than $21 million. Her products are now found in more than 8,000 retailers, including Target, Whole Foods, Trader Joe's. And she's partnered with airlines and hotel chains to expand her offerings. In 2021, Partake Foods closed a $4.8 million Series A funding with 50% of its total funding coming from Black investors, which continues to be her focus.

On LinkedIn, Woodard candidly shared, when Partake was included on *Inc.*'s 5000 List:

> I will be the first to say that this past year has been one of the most challenging I've experienced as a founder—from navigating supply chain hurdles to finding added ways to better our bottom line and build a sustainable business.
>
> Here's what this past year has confirmed for me:
>
> - *Embrace Uncertainty*: Entrepreneurship is a journey—with a capital "J." Getting comfortable with the unknown, strengthening resilience, and adapting quickly are all a part of it.
>   - *Stumble Forward*: Mistakes are valuable learning opportunities that bring you closer to your goals. Short-term setbacks will happen and it's what you do with them that matters most.
>   - *Stay Lean*: Being resourceful (scrappy) and efficient with how you spend your time and money can keep you afloat.
>   - *Build Quality Relationships*: A collaborative network of folks rooting for each other can open doors to partnerships, collaborations, and valuable advice. Surround yourself with people who believe in your vision and truly want to see your brand succeed.

Woodard is unwavering in her commitment to equity and access, from food to financials. Her purpose and alignment give her such tremendous power. The existing rules in both the food and finance industries are blinding paradigms and those first 85 investors did not understand. So she got creative and designed better ones.

Creativity Is Magic

In his book, *Beautiful Economics, A Guide to Gentle World Domination* (2021), Howard Collinge wrote:

> Creativity is the most precious commodity of all. It is almost the most democratic. It can never be owned by one person, corporation or country. It isn't measured by how much money you have, what school you went to or how pretty you are. It is measured by whether your ideas enlighten or improve or inspire. Creativity transcends race, politics, education and culture. It can spring from anywhere. It is the hard, gritty slog of the imagination. Creativity can make the brain spin with possibility or the belly ache with laughter. It can make cities more beautiful and whole populations happier. Creativity knows there's always a better cleaner smarter more generous way. Creativity can make our economy more human, more sustainable, more thoughtful, more useful, more social, more profitable, more lasting and ultimately, more beautiful.

Creativity is something in which anyone can partake, and Woodard, through such incredible tenacity, intelligence, love, and power, as described by Hawkins, continues to demonstrate creativity beautifully.

Rebecca Grynspan, Associate Administrator of the United Nations Development Program (UNDP) said, "If well nurtured, the creative economy can be a source of socio-economic growth, jobs, innovation, and trade, while at the same time, contributing to social inclusion, cultural diversity, and sustainable human development" (Edge Malaysia, 2014).

"New technologies and the internet give developing countries a feasible option to promote their creativity and entrepreneurship in the global market" (dos Santos-Duisenberg, 2010).

Which brings me to funding and the challenges of fundraising and securing capital.

For female founders, it's especially difficult. Last year, female-founded companies raised just 2% of venture capital, according to Pitchbook (Knickerbocker, 2023), a company that provides private market data. That is the lowest level since 2016.

When women can't get access to capital, and if only two cents of every dollar are going to female-led business, it's incredibly common that women resort to bootstrapping and self-funding, which can take a personal toll. According to a Kauffman Foundation survey of nearly 350 female tech founders and startup leaders, 80% reported using personal savings as their primary source of funding to start a business (Klich, 2023).

Today's venture capital is failing female founders. Perhaps it's where the expression "my two cents worth" originated, because that's all the funding they get from each venture capital dollar allocated. But what that means is that "unlike venture-backed companies that can burn through thousands, if not millions, in funding, founders who are relying on their own funds to launch their operation often feel their personal financial decisions are directly tied to the financial decisions of their companies" (Klich, 2023).

Psychotherapist Paul Hokemeyer, Ph.D., whose research focuses on high-performing entrepreneurs, says self-funding has a significant impact on women entrepreneurs' mental health. "This is because women experience a direct connection between the attainment of their financial goals and their personal self-worth," he says (Klich, 2023).

Nonbelievers and Naysayers

This brings me to my friend Arlan Hamilton, who I am convinced in a few years' time will be recognized around the world simply as "Arlan" much like we now recognize "Oprah." She was homeless and sleeping on the floor of the San Francisco airport in 2014. Less than 10 years later, she's the founder of Backstage Capital, a multimillion dollar venture fund.

She shares that in 2014, after cracking her phone screen, she had a callous on her right thumb because she couldn't afford to get the screen fixed and just worked through the pain. She even sometimes wrapped the phone in a Ziploc bag to be able to use it with slightly less pain.

This was all while sharing a hotel room with her mom and figuring out payments day to day, while walking across a four-lane freeway to the grocery store with $10 to figure out several days of food, while planning to launch a multimillion dollar investment firm that would invest in the best and brightest the country had to offer. She shares, "No one understood my vision at the time, but I did. And I could see it as clear as day."

No one understood her vision, but she was undeterred.

According to Knickerbocker (2023) (which I highly recommend you Google and read),

> The venture capital ecosystem is starkly homogenous—long associated with its lack of diversity and representation." In 2020, 8 out of 10 venture capitalists (VC) investment partners were white (Deloitte, Venture Forward, and NVCA, 2021). There's a major lack of investment dollars flowing into Black-founded startups too. Victoria Pettibone (2021) reports that Black women founders are particularly impacted by a lack of funding opportunities—receiving just 0.27% of all U.S. VC dollars since 2018.

According to the U.S. Census Bureau, 58.7% of the U.S. population, age 16 and older, are women. Those who identify as "white alone" are 75.5% and as "Black alone" are 13.6%. So why are Black women founders receiving just 0.27% of all U.S. venture capital dollars? And what about other demographics? Asian/Pacific Islander employees compose 18% of the overall workforce, and the percentage of the overall workforce reported to be Hispanic is 7%.

In a "starkly homogenous" venture capital ecosystem, the white male partners have one lived experience, a paradigm blindness. But Arlan could see that need "clear as day."

And it's now, a decade later, and Arlan is celebrating her second book release and is the founder and managing partner of a multimillion dollar investment fund called Backstage Capital, a seed investment fund that backs overachieving, underrepresented startup founders. She works with Marc Cuban and other powerful investors.

Arlan didn't have a bank account when her first investor wanted to give her $25,000. "Sometimes you don't learn the etiquette, because most of your life has been about surviving," she shared in a PBS interview (Sullivan, 2021). As she reflects on that today, she wonders if she would do the same thing for an up-and-coming entrepreneur. To meet her, you know the answer. As she shares in the PBS interview, "I'm not going to stop someone at the door because they don't know the etiquette."

Arlan funds startup companies that are specifically owned and operated by Women, Black, Latina, and LGBTQ founders, a group of people that typically receive less than 3% of all funding available. Once homeless, she broke into the almost exclusively white male world of venture capital. Her best-selling book, *It's About Damn Time, How to Turn Being Underestimated into Your Greatest Advantage*, published with Rachel Nelson, is based on her personal journey to create the "seemingly impossible." I highly encourage you to read it.

When you talk to her, her focus is so clear: "Did I catalyze someone today, their forward motion? If I did that, I'm good!"

She wanted to invest in 100 companies led by underrepresented founders in five years. She's from Dallas, Texas, and grew up with her mom and brother. In the PBS interview, she describes her upbringing: "A lot of laughter and love in our house. And this very serious poverty we were in." She remembers thinking, "This isn't forever." She goes on to share her thought process, "I envisioned that I would be very wealthy because I had to be. Everybody in the world will know me. My voice is going to be heard by everyone."

An inner knowing, a meaning, gave purpose and power to her life. She shared with me that when she was younger, she would write out "Oprah, Ellen, Arlan." She started as a tour manager, representing acts and networking in an industry that she loved. It was an industry with long hours and an intense work ethic. She asked 100 people in music to work for them. Only one said yes. In other words, that early experience very much paralleled the experience of raising capital. "I never thought of it as just a job, I thought of it as a learning opportunity. An education. Many artists went through Silicon Valley." Arlan did not have a college degree. She had no formal education. So she did her research and learned that about 90% of venture capital was going to white men in a country where they make up only a third of the population. "If I can crack this, can we open this up to a bigger swath of people. Less than 1% goes to people of color. Of all the women in the country, we're sharing less than 10%. Of all of the Black people, we're sharing less than 10%."

How did she begin? "I got flashcards, index cards, wrote out key people, key words, and began quizzing myself. I was so insatiably curious. Even in the beginning, the rejection didn't bother me. Entrepreneurship is like taking two wet sticks, rubbing them together and trying to start a fire."

Self-awareness is an asset. Arlan took a two-week boot camp, while sleeping at the San Francisco airport on rolled up jeans, before meeting Susan Kimberlin. According to Kimberlin's own summary on Crunchbase (n.d.),

> Susan is an angel investor and startup advisor in San Francisco, where she has a front-row seat to an amazing variety of new ventures. She is passionate about making connections and helping people meet their potential.
>
> Kimberlin believes that diversity is an essential and under-utilized asset to all businesses. She focuses on enterprise businesses and technology. Her operational experience spans product development roles from coding to product management at both startups and Fortune 500 companies like PayPal and Salesforce.

Kimberlin was the first person to say yes to Arlan. She offered Arlan $25,000. It was game changing. Arlan didn't have a bank account, so she sent Kimberlin her mom's bank information, and Kimberlin instead helped her set her own account up. Kimberlin then followed on with a second check for $25,000 to set up shop. By 2018, a year ahead of schedule, Arlan's team had invested more than 100 companies. Today, Backstage Capital has invested in more than 200. Arlan's advice? "Bring your true self. Your true self is your best self."

Arlan had years of sacrifice and things not going her way. The entrepreneurial journey is similar. So what does she look for in a founder? "If they're willing to be vulnerable and tell me they don't have it all figured out, it means they are honest." She looks for that kind of candor and vulnerability.

Pitching Your Idea

So what is her advice on how to pitch investors so that your company and idea break through all of the noise? Create compelling comments, emails, and outreach. As Arlan recently shared on LinkedIn:

1. Get to the point
2. Are you pitching the right person?
3. Metrics
4. Build lifetime value, return customer
5. Teach don't preach
6. Be consistent
7. Imagination
8. Ultimately it's about you

This list is full of wisdom. All too often, you see founders ramble on. Time is money, so be deeply respectful of those you speak to. Their time is precious. Make sure your pitch is tight. And remember to ask yourself: How are you adding value?

Arlan often shares, "Money attracts money. You become the asset. Make yourself valuable. The more you know about something the more it allows you to be the commodity. Be the money. I try to emulate [Kimberlin] catalyzing. I am becoming the person I am looking for. It's powerful, humbling and emotional."

Arlan is the first Black noncelebrity woman on the cover of *Fast Company* magazine, following Oprah, Beyonce, and Serena Williams.

As Hawkins wrote in *Power vs, Force*, "Integrity and excellence speak for themselves, because they are aligned with power."

Arlan is power. This story is echoed over and over again by successful entrepreneurs. In a world that encourages conformity and sameness, the fortitude required to carve your own path, to stay true to your unique vision, to build something that has never existed before is so rare. It stands out in a sea of sameness when you are in front of investors, an audience, and employees. Authenticity cannot be duplicated. And you cannot for a moment doubt it. Investors may not agree with your idea, but they will always know exactly what you stand for and who they are dealing with.

The Junk in Your Head

Keep in mind that there is a lot of noise, social conditioning, the media, and a lot of messaging that will influence you. Be aware of what you ingest. We are so mindful of the food we put in our mouths, but the stories we feed our minds, the narratives and messages we put in our heads, are powerfully important when it comes to our intention, success, and the lives we lead.

And yet for so many of us, where cleaning out the junk from our kitchens is easy, cleaning out the junk from our heads is much harder. We keep it in there, feeding it to ourselves, knowing how damaging it can be. We may continue to stay in unhealthy relationships, with those talk about us behind our backs rather than those who have our backs. Why do we do this? Why do we continue to gravitate to those limiting relationships, beliefs, and limiting fears of abandonment, unworthiness, and more?

There is a lot of science behind it actually, and it's the science of familiarity. Brands recognize it, the media recognizes it, and it's at play in our decision-making more than we possibly realize.

The information we choose to consume impacts us on every level. But for many of us, we unconsciously choose what is familiar. And that can be detrimental, both personally and professionally.

And while it's uncomfortable to admit what you don't know, it's one of the most important things you can do for your personal growth and for your business.

So why do we choose familiar? Well, it has a lot to do with psychology.

Shanelle Mullin (2023) wrote, "Unconsciously, we give preference to things and people we're familiar with. Even if the stimuli you're being repeatedly exposed to is negative (e.g., an abusive relationship), you will subconsciously find comfort in the familiarity of it."

It explains the homogeneity of the financial system and the homogeneity in venture capital funding. Venture capitalists, according to the science of familiarity (and perhaps other factors), don't want to risk the unfamiliar.

Mullin goes on, "Psychologists have found that happiness is directly correlated to how many things (e.g. types of music, types of food, activities, countries) we're familiar with."

Why?

"Our brains are lazy," Mullin wrote.

The easier something is to understand, the more likely we are to believe it. According to psychologists, any situation where we are required to weigh information (e.g., voting, buying, marriage) is influenced by cognitive fluency.

If the name of your company is easy to pronounce, shares are likely to perform better.

If you write in a clean, clear font, people are more likely to believe you're stating a fact.

Our brains love prototypes. Once we have an idea of what something should be, we want other similar things to share the same qualities.

Think about it for a minute: cars, skis, refrigerators, water bottles. There is a sameness, a conformity, to all of these categories, and all of the CEOs named "John."

According to Mullins,

Our brains are creatures of habit. If you've ever tried to quit smoking or lose weight, you know this is true. The more often you do something, the more likely it is that you'll continue doing it.

Habits are not easy to change.

All of your habits, good or bad, provide a subconscious benefit to you. That's why they're so difficult to break. You know you shouldn't check your email first thing in the morning because it's bad for productivity, but you do anyway. No matter how hard you try, it's difficult to stop.

Persuading someone to break a habit is very, very difficult.

Also according to Mullin, Amazon Prime members convert at a rate of 74%. When those same Amazon Prime members shop at other online retailers, they convert only 6% of the time on average.

Why? Because the process of purchasing something on Amazon is so familiar to us; it makes it easy, regardless of how new the product might be. The process of going to a new website, keying in information, and learning how to navigate it will prevent that same conversion.

As Mullen shares, "'I got it on Amazon' is almost as popular as 'Google it.' It's become the prototype. As a result, it's become so easy to think about using Amazon that we, well, don't. That's cognitive fluency."

Can it be disrupted? Absolutely. Remember Liquid Death? They successfully challenged the conformity of the bottled water market.

Disrupting Venture Capital Funding

If you apply this to what's happening in venture capital funding, you can see how the issue has become habitual to the point of blindness. You can also see the incredible opportunity that Arlan saw for Backstage Capital.

I learned this too, the science of familiarity, when we were launching our first product at rePlant Capital, which I cofounded back in 2018. Some investors shared feedback: "Make the product you're selling feel familiar." Like Liquid Death, we did, and we didn't. We took something that was familiar (in our case, it was a debt fund, not a beer can) and we adopted it to address the financial challenges confronting farmers in the food industry today.

There is a huge opportunity in the financial industry to create better products. The industry sits where the food industry sat 20 years ago, stale and pale, with a lot of highly processed products. We are so mindful of the products we put in our grocery carts, but what about the products we shop for from financial institutions? Are your investments aligned with your values? Do you even know where your money sleeps at night? Where does it go and to whom when the bank lends it out? It's hard to know. The processing, packaging, and bundling done by financial companies are the equivalent of the ultra-processing now done to so much of the food industry. Better-for-you products exist in the financial sector, products that put your money to work in a way that is aligned with your values, but there is way less advertising around it. And better-for-you banks are emerging, just as better-for-you grocery stores did, banks that are less extractive to your financial health and the health of the planet.

We give a lot of thought into the products that go into our grocery carts, but what about the financial products that we are buying and using, and the banks where we purchase them? How much transparency do you have into that process? How much transparency does your bank give?

Transparency is a superpower. And one thing is certain, if transparency is bad for your business model, you need a new business model.

Action Steps: Blind Spot Inventory

Have you ever been driving in the car, initiated a lane change, only to dramatically have to pull back into your lane because you didn't see a car? That's a blind spot. We are really familiar with that experience. The same thing happens in business. We may initiate an action like we initiate that lane change, thinking we have full information, when in fact we have a blind spot. I want you to write down the times in your life that you have had an "a-ha" moment. When you last learned something new, that was so obvious you can't believe you didn't already know it? And when is the last time you intentionally put yourself into a new situation? The last time you were uncomfortable as the newcomer? It may be everything from starting a new job, learning a new instrument, moving to a new city, or starting an online class.

The point being: for the first few decades of our lives, education is familiar and foundational to our experience. We are students, open to learning. And then, it stops. The invitation is to invite more education back into your life. Where can you learn more about another's experience and upbringing? Where can you expose yourself to new ideas and beliefs? One way that I've tried to do this is to diversify the authors I follow and read, both online and in books. If you look at your bookshelf, you may be surprised to find just how homogenous your author list is. Take a minute to do that. How many male authors do you read? How many female authors? And how many authors from different ethnicities, races, and backgrounds? How many younger writers do you follow online? How many Black writers? Indigenous writers? How many from differing backgrounds do you follow on social media? Take inventory and then take notes. There is so much knowledge and wisdom in others' lived experiences and so much opportunity to expand your own knowledge and learn.

Resources

Celarier, M. (2023). How the Fearless Fund lawsuit is provoking outrage, new DEI strategies—and renewed commitment. *Institutional Investor* [online]. Available at: https://www.institutionalinvestor.com/article /2cdc8zv066plxdq1p83cw/culture/how-the-fearless-fund-lawsuit-is -provoking-outrage-new-dei-strategies-and-renewed-commitment

Collinge, H. (2021). *Beautiful economics: A guide to gentle world domination.* powerHouse Books.

Deloitte, Venture Forward, and NVCA. (2021). *VC human capital survey.* 3rd ed. [online]. Available at: https://www2.deloitte.com/content /dam/Deloitte/us/Documents/audit/vc-human-capital-survey-3rd -edition-2021.pdf

dos Santos-Duisenberg, E. (2010). *United Nations Creative Economy Report 2010.*

Edge Malaysia. (2014). *Creative industries more resilient* [online]. Available at: https://theedgemalaysia.com/article/creative-industries-more-resilient

Fearless Fund. (n.d.). *About* [online]. Available at: https://www.fearless .fund/about (Accessed October 10, 2023).

First Round 10 Year Project. (n.d.). *First Round 10 Year Project* [online]. Available at: http://10years.firstround.com/

Ganesan, V., Mahalingam, R., Nathan, A., Ware, A., and Weinberg, A. (2023). *Underrepresented start-up founders* [online]. McKinsey & Company. Available at: https://www.mckinsey.com/featured-insights /diversity-and-inclusion/underestimated-start-up-founders-the-untapped -opportunity

Girlboss. (2019). *The venture capital world has a problem with women of color* [online]. Available at: https://girlboss.com/blogs/read/venture-capital -woc-women-of-color

Hart, B. (2023). *Bud Light, Target, and a new era of corporate caution* [online]. *Intelligencer.* Available at: https://nymag.com/intelligencer /2023/05/bud-light-target-and-a-new-era-of-corporate-caution.html

Hawkins, D. R. (2006). *Power vs. force: The hidden determinants of human behavior.* Veritas Publishing,

Kimberlin, S. (n.d.). Summary [online]. crunchbase. Available at: https:// www.crunchbase.com/person/susan-kimberlin

Klich, T. B. (2023). Self-funding female founders. *Marie Claire Magazine* [online]. Available at: https://www.marieclaire.com/career-advice/self -funding-female-founders/

Knickerbocker, K. (2023). *82 black founders and investors to watch in 2023* [online]. PitchBook. Available at: https://pitchbook.com/blog/black -founders-and-investors-to-watch#black-investors

Mullin, S. (2023). *The science of familiarity: Increasing conversions by being unoriginal* [online]. CXL. Available at: https://cxl.com/blog/science-of-familiarity/#:~:text=From%20an%20evolutionary%20perspective%2C%20it,want%20to%20risk%20the%20unfamiliar

Olson, A. (2023). A small venture capital player becomes a symbol in the fight over corporate diversity policies. *AP News* [online]. Available at: https://apnews.com/article/fearless-fund-dei-lawsuit-affirmative-action-f6359b2c6596b3ca41111a55e77d20e6

Parsons, A. G. (2023). *Women, philanthropy, and "the great wealth transfer"* [online]. Columbus Foundation. Available at: https://columbusfoundation.org/at-the-table-blog/women-philanthropy-and-the-great-wealth-transfer#:~:text=Women%20are%20poised%20to%20inherit,assets%20in%20the%20United%20States

Pettibone, V. (2023). *VCs must do a better job of supporting black women founders* [online]. TechCrunch+. Available at: https://techcrunch.com/2021/11/03/vcs-must-do-a-better-job-of-supporting-black-women-founders/?guccounter=1&guce_referrer=aHR0cHM6Ly93d3cuZ29vZ2xlLmNvbS8&guce_referrer_sig=AQAAAFtCnwVKNF0rclCqQT7KsH05UtYxH6l67aRa6OIhPiiv4o79YBnFIRSjmoJf3bfb7-zxGdIKTs6Z9a8JBt1X3d_xdPVeXjO0o-D7SM9fBZlRvkUHjo19HYwh3zjdvfsrYrX9IMs8CyM-ZLgPCARLscyhbaD3QU6nwFM1YX2GB0Ip

Shin, R. (2023). Taylor Swift is so important to the economy that she's in the latest Fed report. *Fortune* [online]. Available at:

Sullivan, K. (2021). *Arlan Hamilton. Venture capitalist. Author* [video]. PBS. Available at: https://www.njpbs.org/programs/to-dine-for-with-kate-sullivan/arlan-hamilton-venture-capitalist-author-h92Wws/

Taylor, A. (2023). LinkedIn. Available at: https://www.linkedin.com/posts/followalisont_bud-light-target-and-a-new-era-of-corporate-activity-7069672028428988416-afog/

5

The Liability of Ignorance

"If you're not prepared to be wrong, you'll never come up with anything original."

—Sir Ken Robinson

IN MY FINANCIAL career, I learned how discriminatory our financial system is. It was not something I learned in school. We didn't cover it in college, and we didn't cover it in business school. It's why I include the topic in the course on innovation that I teach at Rice University. Ignorance is a liability. I also never learned a single Native American word in school; although I was given the option to study French, Spanish, Japanese, German, and so many other languages, a Native American language was never offered. I never learned how to say hello or thank you. Where had education failed me on this? Where had I failed myself? And just as I asked you to do at the end of the prior chapter, to explore your sources of information in order to learn what is not familiar to you, I got to work doing the same, in an effort to expand my knowledge and understanding, to address not only my own blindspots, but also the shame I felt over my ignorance. I am and always will be working on this.

Why do I bring this up? Because if we're going to talk about things like fundraising from friends and family, then we have to talk about who has the ability to do this and why and who has generational wealth and who has access to lending. I began learning the depths of the racial discrimination in the financial system, when I first learned that 70% of farmers are white and male. What created that homogeneity? Land was taken from Black and Indigenous families. Assets were taken away. Wealth, like wisdom, gets passed down. But if your grandparents or great grandparents had property stolen from them, they can't pass it down. Generational wealth is a privilege. It's an advantage; it gives you a head start, especially in the fundraising process that often starts with friends and family. It enables you to qualify for loans, to take out debt, to secure an office lease. You have assets to serve as collateral. As I spoke with Black farmers, indigenous farmers, female farmers, and more across the industry, the discrimination that still exists in lending is jaw-dropping.

Until 1988, a woman could not get a business loan without a male relative co-signing. The Women's Business Ownership Act passed to change that. In many cases, legislation is needed to drive out these discriminatory practices, but when 98% of the finance world is governed by one demographic and gender, you don't have that representation in the industry.

The landscape of corporate America is littered with social and environmental initiatives, but unless you get radically honest with the current structures and the legislation beneath them—who they serve and who they fail—and actually understand the history behind them, you will continue to operate with a paradigm blindness and miss both opportunities and risks.

We spend a lot of time getting in physical shape, building on our strengths and addressing our weaknesses. The same opportunity exists with our biases and blindspots. Where are you vulnerable?

Like Arlan did, take yourself to school. This self-education includes understanding not only the intention and the actions of historical racial and gender discrimination but also then identifying your role in it (because no matter the chapter in history, we all play a role, as either a bystander or participant).

Is it comfortable? No. Is it necessary? Absolutely.

The Urinal Lesson

When I started college, the school had been an all-male school for two hundred years. Going co-ed was a huge decision for the alumni, a controversial one at the time that in hindsight looks like a brilliant stroke of genius. But back in the 1980s, it felt anything but. The school was falling in the rankings and found itself losing out to co-ed counterparts, so the vote was made to accept women.

I was in the fifth class of women at the school. The school was five years into the process. And in the dorms, on the female floors, our bathrooms were male bathrooms that still had urinals in them. It was as if to say, we've accepted women; we've met the quota. But we're not going to put too much money into this yet, because we really aren't sure if this is going to stick. We aren't sure if it is going to be the women or the urinals. And many alumni and benefactors were still betting on the urinals, five years into the decision.

A lot of the social and environmental initiatives under way in corporate America today are doing the same. These companies are still bound and attached to the infrastructure that supports one demographic, failing to build out what is needed to support the expanded and necessary inclusion of diversity, equity, sustainability, conservation, and environmental initiatives. Companies, like colleges, can recruit and hit hiring quotas without investing in new infrastructures, and investors are calling it out. *The Financial Times* headlined, "Investors Warns 'Fluffy' ESG Metrics Are Being Gamed to Boost Bonuses." Just like a college board of directors saying, "Look, we're hitting our numbers, we've got women on campus," but hesitating or failing to build out the underlying infrastructure. The same is happening in the C-suite. There is virtue signaling all over the place and press releases are flying, but the underlying investment in the infrastructure still has not been made. Companies are box-ticking. Many efforts are failing, and investors understand the risk.

Dominic Bernard (2022) quoted Michael Ryan, CEO of Dalmore Capital, a London investment company, as saying: "The purpose of a business used to be to generate profits for its shareholders, almost full stop. And if you dared suggest objectives that were not consistent with dividends and profits, you'd be shouted down. But the world has changed. The general view now is that CEOs are accountable to the public."

According to Philippa O'Connor, a national leader of reward and employment practice at PwC UK: "For many investors, and companies, it is precisely because these goals are believed to be in the long-term financial interest of companies that it is important to link them to reward" (Bernard, 2022).

It turns out that "Europe leads the global average for female board representation," according to Beau Jackson (2021), and the 2021 *Credit Suisse Gender 3000* report discovered a diversity premium with companies that had greater gender diversity outperforming companies without it on share price and ESG score. This is not a box-ticking exercise; it is clearly part of leadership's fiduciary duty to not only hire more diverse candidates, but also to build out the resources needed to retain them. It's good for business. Rewarding executives for hitting hiring quotas but not for metrics on retention and promotion of diversity of teams makes this a short-term, bonus-boosting exercise and not a long-term solution. Which is what is upsetting investors, because the data about the outperformance of these teams, the ones who meaningfully embrace diversity into their core values and actions, are so compelling.

Remember that earlier statistic about outperformance? Racially diverse founding teams outperform their peers, returning 30% more capital to investors when they reach exit by acquisition or IPO.

And public companies with female CEOs outperformed the stock price of those with male CEOs by 20% within the first two years of a woman taking leadership.

It's your fiduciary duty to drive returns for investors. If this is the data, then why does the venture capital industry and the basic infrastructure of most companies still favor one demographic? There is paradigm blindness, familiarity bias, and conformity at play.

Where can you build out better? How can you invest in the infrastructure to support a more diverse workforce? You can't just change the numbers without also investing in changing the infrastructure. What basic needs are not being met? What flexibility is needed? What support is needed? What holidays are important? What traditions? What's expected? What's assumed? This goes so much deeper than the number in the C-suite. It requires learning new information, adopting the mindset of a student, and tabling pride. It should be something that is required of leaders.

As Ray Dalio says, "You learn. You change your mind. It's called growing."

I am reminded of a dear friend who called one day from one of the large multinational food companies. The leadership team there was homogenous, and she'd been called out for her shoes. Apparently, her shoes did not conform. There was no room for variation, no understanding of a different experience or culture, no curiosity, just a command handed down.

"That's wrong," I said. She knew it; I knew it. Her family knew it. Her friends knew it. And within months, she'd left and gone on to a powerful leadership role at a female-founded company, where she now inspires millions, filling her social media feeds with so much authenticity and color, beautifully successful in her career. And her shoes? Professional, colorful, and amazing.

Listen to Learn

So why am I telling you this? Because the expression, "to step into someone else's shoes" is an important part of business. We do it all the time when we are thinking about the experience of the customer. It needs to happen more when it comes to expanding and diversifying our teams.

It is a reminder to practice empathy, and yet empathy is not often part of a leadership team's evaluation. It should be.

We don't know what we don't know. We have inherent blind spots, absolutely every single one of us, regardless of race or gender, because of the lived experience we've had. But if we are going to meet the changing needs of the twenty-first century consumer, and the changing demands of the market and environment, we need teachers and allies to build resiliency, to bring in experts, and to listen and learn.

If we're going to talk about things like "biodiversity" in the twenty-first century, which everyone from Fidelity Institutional to the United Nations is now doing, and the impacts of business on the planet, then we can't continue to ignore the fact that the word "diversity" is hiding in plain sight in the middle of the word "biodiversity."

In fact, the word "biodiversity" doesn't exist without "diversity," so we need to do a much better job integrating it into business models, from integrating indigenous wisdom and leadership on farms to adding WoC to boards, to diversifying everything from venture capital to cap tables.

As Arlan Hamilton of Backstage Capital shared, "Ignoring the experience of 70% of the population will set your company up for failure. Failing to capture that diversity of experience and knowledge will prove to be a shortcoming."

So how do you get familiar with demographics and consumers you may not know? And how do you expand your network to include a diverse group of leaders, experiences, and knowledge?

You put your ego into your back pocket. You embrace humility and curiosity and get to work.

You teach yourself what you may not have been taught, you unlearn to relearn, and you listen. It requires deep humility to realize that there is a lot of unlearning of social conditioning to do and a lot of learning, listening, and empathy that needs to happen.

And that requires refamiliarizing yourself with being a student. It requires embracing the unfamiliar. And remember our bias toward the familiar? You're going to have to challenge that familiarity bias and grab a pack of index cards like Arlan did, your phone, a computer, and learn. Films, groups, community organizations, churches, documentaries, music, cultural organizations, and events are great places to start. Get comfortable being uncomfortable. It's good for relationship building, it's good for partnerships, it's good for business.

Don't Shrink and Pink

A report called "Finding Alpha: The Trillion Dollar Female Economy," authored by Cake Ventures, which is led by Monique Woodard, includes the following:

> Women control or influence over 85% of consumer spending, including healthcare for themselves and their children,

consumer retail, household needs, and more. In spite of this market-making influence and purchasing power, women have long been treated as a niche market whose needs can be met by 'shrinking and pinking' products originally designed for men. Women are responsible for more than $31 trillion in yearly consumer spending.

The female consumer of today is markedly different—and more influential—than ever before. In 2023, TikTok's global user base was 60% female and 40% male.

Today, women make up the majority of college students, 59.5%, with men representing 40.5% of college students. And while overall enrollment in U.S. universities is declining, men account for 71% of that decline. If this trend continues, soon two women will earn a college degree for every one man.

Expanding workforce participation coupled with an increase in education has led to a growth of women's wages. Between 1979–2019, women's wages increased significantly, although not uniformly: for white women wages increased 39%, for Black women wages increased 27%, and Latinas saw an increase of 24%. This has all translated into a dramatic increase in women's financial power. American women control more than $10 trillion in assets (an amount expected to triple in the next decade), driven by a continuation of these changes: workforce participation, education, and wage growth—alongside generational wealth transfer and increasing financial decision-making power. (Bugay, 2023)

If that doesn't sum up a powerful opportunity, I am not sure what else does.

As women gain economic strength and more education, they insist on equity, equality, inclusion, justice, and more. Hispanic women will represent 25% of the population by 2050. However, less than 2% of C-suite positions and board seats go to Latinas. The U.S. Latino economy continues to grow, reaching $3.2 trillion in 2021. If Latinos were an individual country, their GDP would rank fifth in the world, ahead of the United Kingdom, India, and France. Does your leadership team reflect this? So much is changing, affording so many new opportunities, and yet so many business practices remain the same, from venture capital funding to childcare.

The Missing Infrastructure

Childcare has long been a dilemma for working parents. It keeps parents out of the workplace, and it prevents women from returning to work after the birth of a child. It's also been a key piece of infrastructure that's been missing, as efforts get under way on representation, equity, inclusion, and justice. If you want to send a clear and meaningful signal that you are serious about inclusivity, invest in infrastructure and programs that reflect it.

It's like building women's bathrooms on an all-male campus—it sends a strong signal that you are serious about supporting women and not just checking a box.

So why do so few companies do it?

According to Power to Fly (Smalley, n.d.), "Offering good childcare benefits is one of the top ways employers can combat the pay gap, but it's also simply good for business: studies have shown that offering childcare benefits can reduce absenteeism by as much as 30%, and turnover by up to 60%." This extends to parental and pet care too, as not everyone has children.

However, as shared by Patagonia (2016), "Every day in America, women return to work after the birth of a child to find an unsupportive environment lacking onsite childcare, lactation programs, and paid medical leave. No wonder there is an alarming lack of women in positions of leadership, board rooms, and public office.

Women will never be able to effectively 'lean in' without the proper economic, social, and community support for the most critical work of all: raising the next generation."

Every single one of us is on this planet because a woman was strong enough to put us here.

Patagonia has been offering onsite childcare for its employees for 30 years. I remember the first time I saw it at their Ventura campus—it was stunning and so obvious. The CFO at the time, Phil Graves, proudly shared how he brings his daughters to work with him, and then checks in with them throughout the day. And I thought, "Why isn't every company providing this? A company will invest millions in an onsite gym that hardly gets used. Why not invest in something that benefits every working parent?"

Onsite childcare, especially for infants, is a critical element of doing business in our time—and it's proven to be good for business. Now, more than 30 years later, companies like Hormel are following Patagonia's lead. And some companies are shifting gears entirely, as post-pandemic life takes shape, with more teams working remotely, offering flexible childcare benefits.

It was Yvon Chouinard's wife, Malinda, who first introduced onsite childcare at Patagonia. The data supporting this investment are significant.

When Yvon Chouinard, Patagonia's iconic founder, and his wife Malinda started the company, their employees were friends and family, and they wanted to support them as they worked and started their families. The solution was not to fix a problem, but to respond to what humans need, including a place to nurse newborns and, later, to provide safe and stimulating childcare. The results three decades later are not surprising: 100% of the women who have had children at Patagonia over the past five years have returned to work, significantly higher than the 79% average in the United States. About 50% of managers are women, and 50% of the company's senior leaders are women.

"We wonder why in corporate America women are absent at these levels," Rose Marcario, Patagonia's former CEO, said. But the answer is really not that difficult, or expensive, she says. "You have to value care-giving."

According to the Organization for Economic Cooperation and Development, out of 41 countries, the United States is the only one that does not mandate any paid leave for new parents. Only about 16% of employers offer fully paid maternity. Things don't get easier after the babies are born. According to a report from Care.com, the majority of low- or middle-income families spend more than 10% of their household income on childcare and one-fifth spends 20%. One study actually found that in 23 states, full-time preschool for four-year-olds was more expensive that in-state public college tuition. Those policy choices have consequences. Only 69% of women return to work a year after giving birth, down from a peak of 74% in 1999. The United States is one of the only developed countries in which that figure is falling; in Britain, France, and Germany, the numbers have increased dramatically.

Patagonia's Ventura childcare center costs about $1 million a year to run, not including tuition fees or the costs parents pay. It employs 28 staff and another five at a customer service and distribution plant in Reno. The two sites serve 80 kids. The Ventura site recoups 91% of the cost ($500,000 through tax breaks, 30% through the value of retention, and 11% in employee engagement). As a percentage of all selling, general, and administrative costs, it is 0.005%. This does not seem prohibitive.

It comes back to values. How we spend our money is the truest indicator of what we value. Do you value employee retention? Diversity in leadership? Gender equity? Are you addressing basic human needs for women? Your company's actions speak louder than any words in a press release. And onsite childcare telegraphs those values and meets those needs. Thankfully, other companies like Dow Jones, Intuit, Expedia, and others are following suit.

Others offer a Benefits Wallet, to be used for childcare, parent care, or pet care.

In a *Wall Street Journal* article by Rachel Feintzeig (2016), some companies are catching on. Some offer onsite care (often outsourced to a specialist childcare provider like Bright Horizons). Home Depot's corporate campus offers 66,000 square feet of indoor and outdoor space, with three playgrounds, a basketball court and a water park (Feintzeig, 2016). Other companies are offering flexible childcare benefits, as more employees continue to work remotely.

Netflix offers unlimited paid parental leave for a year following the birth or adoption of a child, besting Facebook, which was the parental leave champion, with four months of paid parental leave. At Alphabet-owned Google and YouTube, birth mothers get 18 weeks of paid leave (during which their stock shares vest).

It's not only good for mothers; it's great for dads and the bottom line too. An average business with 250 employees can save $75,000 per year in lost work time by subsidizing care for employees' sick children (Reed and Clark, 2004).

U.S. companies lose $3 billion annually as a consequence of childcare-related absences, estimates the Child Care Action Campaign (Elswick, 2003). And 85% of employers report that providing childcare services improves employee recruitment.

But as I write this, beginning September 30, 2023, states face a steep drop-off in federal childcare investment. Without Congressional action, this cliff will have dire consequences. More than three million children are projected to lose access to childcare nationwide. Seventy thousand childcare programs are likely to close. This will have ripple effects for parents forced out of work or to cut their work hours, for businesses who will lose valuable employees or experience the impact of their employees' childcare disruptions, and state economies that will lose tax revenue and jobs in the childcare sector as a result.

Shelley Zalis, founder and CEO of the Female Quotient, noted on her LinkIn page that more U.S. women are working than ever before. The participation rate for women ages 25–54 climbed to a record high of 77.5% in April, surpassing a peak reached in 2000. Federal childcare funding ($24 billion) expired September 30, which helped childcare programs offer higher wages to attract staff, could leave 3.2 million children without daycare. Parents, and especially mothers, will face a choice: work fewer hours or leave the workforce altogether.

Investments Are Values on Display

American women control more than $10 trillion in assets (an amount expected to triple in the next decade), driven by a continuation of these changes: workforce participation, education, and wage growth, alongside generational wealth transfer and increasing financial decision-making power. Their power is growing, and if companies aren't providing these benefits, addressing basic human needs, they'll lose talent.

In 2022, companies with one or more female founders raised $44.6 billion in venture capital. Still, in 2022, only 16.3% of venture capital went to companies with at least one female founder and all-women teams received only 2.1% of venture capital, with Black women and Latinas raising less than 1% of venture capital combined.

Even with less access to capital, in 2022, there were 83 female-founded private companies valued at $1 billion or more, and companies with at least one female founder created over $57 billion in exit value.

Public companies with female CEOs outperformed the stock price of those with male CEOs by 20% within the first two years of a woman taking leadership. Yet, in 2021—a year that broke the record for the most IPOs led by women—still, only 0.01% of all U.S. IPOs were led by female CEOs.

Read that again. In 2021, only 0.01% of all U.S. IPOs were led by female CEOs, despite the fact that public companies with female CEOs outperformed the stock price of those with male CEOs by 20% within the first two years of a woman taking leadership.

Is a familiarity bias impacting fiduciary duty? Paradigm blindness? Intentional ignorance? Is it a failure in infrastructure, or a lack of investment in childcare options? More?

The data are compelling and clear. Diversity in the C-suite is good for your bottom line. If a product generated 20% more revenue, wouldn't you promote it? So why aren't we doing that and getting more women into C-suite roles and leadership positions? And why aren't we changing the infrastructure to support them when the data are this clear? It clearly impacts profits.

Ask yourself, "Which companies are not influenced by the female dollar?" "What does a woman need in the workplace that is different from male needs?" "What flexibility may be required?" "Do you have women on your board who can speak to this experience?" And think about this as basic human needs, not accommodations to the male experience, but as the unique physical needs that women have. Every single person is on this planet, every employee, every investor and customer, because a woman was strong enough to deliver them here. There is so much power in that, so much strength and fortitude, and building a business model that supports women—as employees, board members, and customers—is good for your bottom line. Full stop.

Action Steps: Values Inventory

We are going to call this one the *values inventory*. It'll get pretty honest pretty quickly. I want you to take inventory of the gender diversity you have in your organization. What programs do you have in place? What infrastructure? Do you have childcare? Nursing rooms? Do you have time off for caregivers? For aging parents or children? Do your competitors? What about retention of women? Do they come back after they've had a baby? Do they leave? And if some of these questions make you uncomfortable, ask yourself why. What blind spots do you have? What biases? We all have them, but when we build out a diverse team, our collective experience minimizes them.

Resources

Anderson, J. (n.d.). *This is what work-life balance looks like at a company with 100% retention of moms* [online]. Available at: http://tony-silva.com/eslefl/miscstudent/downloadpagearticles/patagonia-workingmoms-quartz.pdf

Bernard, D. (2022). Rise in CEOs linking pay to engagement and diversity targets. *HR Magazine* [online]. Available at: https://www.hrmagazine.co.uk/content/news/rise-in-ceos-linking-pay-to-engagement-and-diversity-targets/

Bugay, B. (2023). *Finding alpha: The trillion dollar female economy.* [online]. Cake Ventures. Available at: https://assets.website-files.com/62eadeaa175d45804906da28/6451cf78d4b56780ff09e34b_Finding%20Alpha%20-%20The%20Trillion%20Dollar%20Female%20Economy%20-%20Report.pdf?mod=article_inline

Elswick, J. (2003, June 15). More employers offer back-up care. *Employee Benefit News* [online]. Available at: http://www.accessmylibrary.com/coms2/summary_0286-23549740_ITM.

Feintzeig, R. (2016, Sept. 26). The case for day care at the office. *Wall Street Journal* [online]. Available at: https://www.wsj.com/articles/the-case-for-day-care-at-the-office-1474882201

Jackson, B. (2021). Europe leads global average for female board representation. *HR Magazine* [online]. Available at: https://www.hrmagazine.co.uk/content/news/europe-leads-global-average-for-female-board-representation

Jordan, H. (2017). Long-term focus and meaningful CSR will bring profit. *HR Magazine* [online]. Available at: https://www.hrmagazine.co.uk/content/news/long-term-focus-and-meaningful-csr-will-bring-profit

Patagonia. (2016). *We can be both: Mothers at work* [Video]. Medium. Available at: https://patagonia.medium.com/we-can-be-both-mothers-at-work-2cdb47730df1

Reed P. S. and Clark, S. M. (2004). *Win-win workplace practices: Improved organizational results and improved quality of life*. U.S. Department of Labor Women's Bureau.

Smalley, A. (n.d.). *15 companies with great childcare benefits for working parents* [online]. PowerToFly. Available at: https://powertofly.com/up/companies-with-great-childcare-benefits

6

Imposter Syndrome and "Not Enough-ness"

"Only the truth of who you are, if realized, will set you free."

—Eckhart Tolle

WHEN I SAT down with my friend Jessica Yellin, who was the chief White House correspondent at CNN, I was again reminded of how many invisible hands are at play in the market and how the media influences not only how we feel about ourselves but also what we learn and even what we do.

Have you ever spent an hour scrolling on Instagram only to realize that you feel absolutely terrible after doing it? I call it the "not enough-ness syndrome." There's a reason for it.

But first, I want to share a little bit of data about these platforms because of how relevant they are for business.

A staggering 94% of consumers engage with some sort of social platform at least monthly—a sign of the huge opportunities present for brands in this space. The average consumer also spends 37% of their time online on social media, making it a good place to reach a large audience of people.

On top of this, more are turning to social media to find products—the number who find out about new brands and products through social media advertising has grown 9% since Q1 2020. It was only being beaten by ads on music streaming services by one percentage point.

Negativity Bias in Your Brain

According to Tom Casey (2022), "Engagement is the currency of social media platforms, and driving engagement involves recommending content and users of interest. Recommender systems use data, computing power, and machine learning to get a user's attention and keep them engaged. The better a platform's algorithms are at keeping users engaged, the more the platform can tout its value to advertisers. In 2020, the global market for digital advertising and marketing was estimated at $350 billion, and it is expected to more than double by 2026 to $768 billion (Casey, 2022). This is in large part a result of increased engagement. According to a Pew Research Center report from March 2021, 85% of Americans go online daily, and nearly a third of adults are online "constantly" (Perrin and Atske, 2021)."

It turns out that social media models use negativity to drive engagement. So no, you're not making it up when you notice that you feel demonstrably worse after scrolling for too long. In fact, we've all experienced this. Have you ever said something that you totally regretted? Did you make a mistake that you can't shake? Forget to highlight a key and critical point in a presentation, only to then be criticized for it? Our brains latch onto these experiences. And social media platforms take advantage of this wiring. The algorithms then feed us content that reinforces that negativity, creating what is called a *confirmation bias*. Breaking that negativity loop takes work. It's a bad habit that you can replace with a better one. This took me some time to figure out, but it's a really important part of leadership. When your brain goes into these negative thought patterns, step back from them and try to notice them. You are literally feeding yourself negative thoughts. Your body is hearing everything you say to yourself.

We are so mindful of the food we put in our mouths; we need to do the same with the thoughts we put in our heads.

According to Casey (2022), "Regardless of whether this is an explicit objective, any effective recommender system that is designed to drive engagement will ultimately unlock the inherent biological triggers of negative bias. The impacts are only now starting to be fully realized, but this suggests a cycle with very real, detrimental effects:

- Exposing end users to content that reinforces unhealthy pre-dispositions and encourages development of harmful ideas that would otherwise not have manifested,
- Encouraging people to bypass the typical inquiry-based learning process by which ideas and content are independently explored; instead relinquishing the supply of information to the recommender system, whereby,
- More personalized feedback based on personal behavior is delivered without context; thus, unlocking innate negative triggers more effectively and ultimately increasing an overall desire to stay engaged.
- Repeat the cycle . . . "

He goes on to call for action from users themselves, the social media platforms, policy makers, advertisers, and academics.

According to Csaba Szabo (2023), EMEA Managing Director, Integral Ad Science (IAS), "Despite the concern of eroding consumer trust in social platforms, our own research shows that more than nine-in-ten of the industry (91%) plan to advertise on social platforms in 2023. The high rates of consumer usage, ad engagement, and the continued growth of influencer marketing is still a pull for advertisers."

So ultimately, like the food you choose to consumer, your media diet is on you too. Be aware of the content you consume. Understand that there is a negativity bias at play to keep you hooked. Do not believe every thought you have. Stop and question them; ask yourself if they are serving you or holding you back. Movies have content ratings like G, PG, PG-13, R, and X. Should other media platforms? Which brings me back to my friend, Jessica Yellin, who is, in some ways, an experienced combination of all of the above.

Talking Heads and Algorithms

Focused primarily on politics, Jessica Yellin was the chief White House correspondent for CNN in Washington, D.C., from 2011 to 2013. She was described as "one of the most powerful women in Washington" and began reporting for CNN as the network's senior political correspondent in 2007, covering Capitol Hill, domestic politics, and the White House. Her book, *Savage News*, was published in April 2019.

Yellin joined CNN as a Capitol Hill correspondent in August 2007. As chief White House correspondent, she conducted in-depth interviews of President Barack Obama, Secretary of State Hillary Clinton, First Lady Michelle Obama, former White House Chief of Staff Rahm Emanuel, House Speaker John Boehner, and former top economist Larry Summers. Prior to serving as chief White House correspondent, Yellin served as national political correspondent at CNN, where she traveled the country covering hotly contested races throughout the network's 2008 and 2012 "America

Votes" election coverage. Yellin has also covered significant policy debates in Washington, D.C., including the push to reform the financial regulatory system.

The media has a powerful influence over the markets, consumer sentiment, and so much more. With a single story, it can move markets and shape the narrative. Food poisoning, corruption, scandals, affairs? The media is the first to inform us. Everything that you use as a channel, whether it's CNN or TikTok, that usage becomes data that are then packaged, bundled, and sold.

It's why sitting down with someone who has firsthand experience in shaping the news was so fascinating. Any time a product is free to us as consumers, like the media or social media, it's important to remember that we are in fact the product. Our eyeballs, our data, our habits, and our patterns are what is being sold. Advertisers buy access to that data and information. So while you may think that you are CNN's customer (or Fox, ESPN, Instagram, TikTok, or any of the media networks), you're not. The companies buying the ads on these networks are the companies' customers. The networks sell our views, habits, and data to advertisers. We are not the media companies' clients; the advertisers are.

The influence that advertisers have over television, print, journals, and the media has been acknowledged for hundreds of years. In 1970, Stanley Cohen wrote about television's dilemma of trying to serve the public on one hand while selling that public to the advertiser on the other. In other words, this has been going on for a long time.

Jessica's career was fed by curiosity and a genuine need to understand. She felt a sense of obligation to give that information to viewers. She wanted to do well and do good, to provide answers to the public. She interned in college on the second floor of the West Wing, when TVs hung in the corners with fish wire and the only 24/7 news channel was CNN.

"I saw the politicians as 'just people,'" she said when we spoke in August 2023. "And when news broke, suddenly everyone in the room would turn towards the box in the corner." She said the entire room would stop, and everyone would turn to face the television.

"I wanted to be in the box," she said.

At the time, she was drawn toward the nexus of single moms, childcare, early education, and support needed to move people out of poverty and into the middle class. We'd call it "welfare reform" today, but what she was actually focused on was building the scaffolding to lift people out of poverty. She was focused on human needs.

"Poverty and rural areas aren't popular topics in the media" she said. "And as a White House intern, I knew I wanted to be one of the people in the box." Listening to her, I couldn't help but realize that we had "influencers" before we had influencers. She was one of them. Today, they are the talking heads on all of our screens.

But as her career continued, she realized you not only had to pay your dues, but you began to adapt to the system, to do what it takes to succeed.

"It's a very unhealthy environment," she said.

And she relayed a story where, in high school, she'd had to introduce Bella Abzug, who was always willing to say what people needed to hear, even if it was unpopular. Bella Savitzky Abzug, nicknamed "Battling Bella," was an American lawyer, politician, social activist, and a leader in the women's movement. When Jessica shared that her interests had been anchored so early in her life, I asked if she'd always had this sense of moral obligation and who instilled these values in her.

"My dad," she said. "He lived them. Do well, do good. 'Tikkun olam.' It's an expression that means 'to heal the world.'"

Her courage is rare, as she stepped away from a system that she felt was unhealthy. As we sat down together, what she shared was fascinating.

Before cable television, there were three channels. Most stations carried the same stories. Today, the news is more of an op-ed, an interpretation, and it blasts news that is mostly negative, throughout the day.

Jessica shared the motivation behind the negativity, again pointing to "negativity bias" and how it hooks us.

According to an article on *Psycom* (Jaworski, 2020), our proclivity for paying attention to negative rather than positive information is an evolutionary hand-me-down from our cave-dwelling ancestors. Back then, alertness to danger, a.k.a., "the bad stuff," was a matter of life and death.

"We inherited the genes that predispose us to give special attention to those negative aspects of our environments that could be harmful to us," explains psychologist and happiness researcher Timothy J. Bono, PhD, who teaches a course in the Science of Happiness at Washington University in St. Louis. In this way, dwelling on the "bad stuff" is similar to the sensation of pain—it's our bodies working to keep us safe.

Moreover, negative emotions rouse the amygdala, the almond-shaped brain structure that psychologist Rick Hansen, PhD, founder of the Wellspring Institute for Neuroscience and Contemplative Wisdom, calls "the alarm bell of your brain." According to Dr. Hansen, the amygdala "uses about two-thirds of its neurons to look for bad news. Once it sounds the alarm, negative events and experiences get quickly stored in memory, in contrast to positive events and experiences, which usually need to be held in awareness for a dozen or more seconds to transfer from short-term memory buffers to long-term storage."

Think about that for a minute (or 12 seconds). We are biologically wired to react differently to negative stimulation. The negative stuff goes straight into your memory. The positive stuff? It needs to be held for 12 or more seconds to transfer from short-term memory into long-term storage. It's why you can still remember exactly where you were when the Space Shuttle blew up or someone died. It sticks. We remember the negative, which then makes us less likely to expose ourselves and risk rejection again.

But entrepreneurship has both risk and rejection baked in. For every story I've shared, the founder has recounted the hundreds of rejections received before getting to "yes." So how do we override this negativity bias and the constant rejection? (Remember Denise at Partake had almost 90 nos from investors before her first yes?)

According to Jaworski (2020), "Not only do negative events and experiences imprint more quickly, but they also linger longer than positive ones, according to researcher Randy Larsen, PhD. In other words, for a multitude of reasons, including biology and chemistry, we're more likely to register an insult or negative event than we are to take in a compliment or recall details of a happy event."

You can probably remember with acute clarity the times you've put your foot in your mouth or screwed something up, regardless of whether it was 10 minutes ago or 10 years ago. And it turns out that women are more likely to internalize negative emotions, getting either sad or depressed or both, and men are more likely to externalize, getting angry.

So the news cycle is impacting our mood cycle. You're not crazy, but once you know that, you can do something about it and manage your intake, much like you would food that is unhealthy for you.

But there is good news, according to Jaworski: "Despite the evolutionary hand we've been dealt, the degree to which we're able to override our 'default' setting and avoid falling into an abyss of self-recrimination, insecurity, sadness, anger, bitterness, and other negative emotions depends on a slew of factors." Those factors include our upbringing (back to that voice in your head), the input we've received from those around us whose opinions we value (like my friend Alex Bogusky), and how we interpret what we've been told.

The most important thing that we can do—and believe me, I understand how big this ask is—is to change the way that we talk to ourselves about our experiences. Something that really helped me change the negative self-talk was to shine a light on it, expose it, as if I was speaking the words out loud to someone that I love. I would never speak to someone I love the way that I was speaking to myself. Would you? Would you ever use that critical tone with a friend, a child or a loved one? I hope not. So why speak to yourself that way?

The Voice in Your Head

I want you to stop for a minute and think about how you talk to yourself in your own head.

Do you have a positive or critical voice? Whose voice do you hear? Is it someone else's? A spouse or a parent? Is it your own? A coach? A teacher? A naysayer? Our upbringings, according to Jaworski—our birth order, our experiences—play such a powerful role in that voice in our head.

Now ask yourself, "Is this how I want to speak to myself now that I am an adult?" Chances are that this is not how you'd choose to speak to yourself as an adult or anyone else for that matter, especially as an entrepreneur. Create a little space between you and that voice, and begin to question it and interrupt it.

As Grant Brenner, MD, Adjunct Assistant Clinical Professor of Psychiatry, Mt. Sinai Beth Israel Medical Center (New York), provides the following advice:

Be poised to gently recognize what is happening when negative patterns start to get activated and practice doing something each and every time—even something very small—to break the pattern. If you are inclined to overanalyze parts of conversations that you assume are negative, figure out a hobby or habit that keeps you from overanalyzing, like reading, going for a run, cleaning your house up, or creating a music playlist that makes you feel happy.

Notice your negative self-dialogue and substitute positive approaches. "You idiot!" becomes, "I wish I had made a different choice, but I will remember how I wish I had acted and apply it to future situations." Another tactic that might feel strange at first, but can help to approach your mean inner voice with kindness, is talking to yourself as you would a friend. When negative thoughts intrude, ask yourself, "Are you okay? What's wrong? Why are you so angry? Are you feeling hurt?" (Jaworski, 2020).

The idea is to good-naturedly interrupt yourself whenever you start to trash talk yourself, because sometimes our toughest critic is the one between our own ears.

The STOP Protocol

When I hear that negative voice in my own head, I've learned to stop a pause and ask if I'd allow anyone that I love to speak to themselves that way. The answer is always no. We can be our own worst critic. The meanest bully may often be the voice in your own head. Stop. Question it. Pause it and do everything you can to disrupt it. Would you ever speak to someone you love that way? Hopefully not. To help you get a handle on this, I developed something I call the "STOP protocol":

S: Suspend the voice. Bring it to a standstill. Silence it.
T: Tone-police yourself. Would you ever speak to someone else this way?
O: Offer a kinder viewpoint, the way you would to a loved one.
P: Patiently remind yourself that you are unwinding a lifetime of negativity bias.

Eleanor Roosevelt said, "No one can make you feel inferior without your consent." And maybe, you *were* made to feel inferior and weren't in a position to give consent. But now, you very much are in control, so get curious about the critical voice in your head and what may be feeding it.

Why? Because, as Deion Sanders says, "You've got to believe to succeed."

Not Enough-ness Syndrome

As you build out the infrastructure around you, it is so important to be incredibly mindful of not only the people you surround yourself with, but also the thoughts you're constructing in your mind and the media that you are consuming. Anything that is created has supportive scaffolding around it during its construction. You as a leader, as an entrepreneur, are no different. Intentionally placing the very best supportive scaffolding around you is going to have a profound effect on your strength, fortitude, vision, tenacity, determination, and the construction and design of what you're building. Your thoughts and beliefs are part of your scaffolding.

But what I call "not enough-ness syndrome" can do a number on anyone. It's when the naysayers in your head get loud. The author Cleo Wade articulated it perfectly when she wrote, "Enoughness is not a mountain. It's a mirage of a mountain. We do not need to climb it. We need to see through it."

One of the best practices that I've put in place during challenging times, either personally or professionally, is what I call the "open ask." It usually happens when I am struggling with a challenge or situation. When I get into bed at night, I literally ask what lesson I am meant to be learning during that hardship or challenge and to learn it quickly, so that I can move through it and back into action. As I lay in bed, I picture my heart opening to learning the lesson.

And I always ask to learn it quickly, because those growing pains can be tough!

Once you start to see challenges as opportunities for learning and growth, you see through them, and they become far less intimidating. They can pull you down, for sure. Remember, I call this the "slingshot theory." Often you will find yourselves getting pulled backward, like a slingshot, before you excel forward. Challenges and mistakes are the lessons for success. They help you to develop some of your most valuable strengths and skills.

Imagine building an office tower without supportive scaffolding. Imagine trying to build healthy self-esteem without strong support. If you have people around you who are constantly tearing you down, let them know how their lack of support is impacting you. If they refuse to change, find new people to fill your inner circle. That human scaffolding that you have around you matters as much as the scaffolding that goes around a building as it is designed. It can either fuel your strength or your fears. Choose wisely.

Don't build a business without a supportive infrastructure either, from childcare to pet care, to mental health benefits in place for your employees, to the advisors and board that you assemble to guide you, to the thoughts, literature, and media you consume. You want to keep the junk out of your head and minimize blind spots as much as possible.

Action Steps: Naysayer Inventory

So how do you ensure against toxicity and build the very best practices?

For the exercise at the end of this chapter, I want you to make a *naysayer inventory*. Get super candid about the negativity in your life. Again, no one needs to see this. What matters is that you are radically honest with yourself. Because just like the fear and shame inventory at the beginning, the naysayers are going to weigh you down. If you let yourself, you will spend precious time and energy defending yourself from their attacks, which is time and energy that you are not spending on building your vision and creating solutions. Naysayers will no doubt be peppering you with multiple worst-case-scenario models, and you could spend the rest of your life refuting them, their hypotheticals, and their what-ifs.

Or you could get down to the business of building better. Because just as you can't drive a car forward while looking in the rearview mirror, you can't prepare for the best if you are preparing for the worst.

One has positive energy and power; the other does not. It's like smiling and frowning. You are going to have to choose one and move accordingly.

As Rich Roll shared on his podcast,

> It's crucial if you're going to navigate this journey that you have to do an adequate amount of internal excavation to kind of understand yourself. Like what is the narrative you're walking about with that is dictating your behavior? And is that true? Get into your past trauma and how they're triggering unhelpful behavior patterns time and time again.
>
> Because there is an unconscious kind of operating system here that will persist without that kind of work. If you're not actually reckoning with all of that, you're unlikely to claw out of whatever paradigm you're in and reorg your life around a better trajectory.

And if you don't yet know Rich Roll, I highly suggest listening to his podcast. On his website, he shares his story, "a graduate of

Stanford University and Cornell Law School, Rich is a 50-year old, accomplished vegan ultra-endurance athlete and former entertainment attorney turned full-time wellness & plant-based nutrition advocate, popular public speaker, husband, father of 4 and inspiration to people worldwide as a transformative example of courageous and healthy living." He is also very honest about his recovery from alcohol and drug use, and what fueled his passion to change his life. His candor is refreshing and gives others permission to do the same.

So I want you to bravely build a list of the negative forces in your life—the patterns, habits, and people. Then also build a list of the positive influences in your life—the things that bring you joy, energy, ambition, and positivity. Think of them as your encouragement and your reinforcement when things get rough.

In one column, you have the Shacklers and in the other the Supporters. Get really honest with the people, behaviors, and habits. Just as you try to minimize and reduce your exposure to the junk food that isn't good for your health, you're going to work on the same thing here—minimizing your exposure to the people who aren't good for your mental health.

Resources

Casey, T. (2022). Rethinking engagement: Challenging the financial model of social media platforms. *Harvard Data Science Review*. doi: https://doi.org/10.1162/99608f92.f09b190b

Cohen, S. E. (1970). The advertiser's influence in TV programming. *Osgoode Hall Law Journal*, 8(1), pp. 91–117. doi: https://doi.org /10.60082/2817-5069.2342

Jaworski, M. (2020). *The negativity bias: Why the bad stuff sticks and how to overcome it* [online]. Psycom.net. Available at: https://www.psycom .net/negativity-bias

Szabo, C. (2023). *Social advertising in 2023: What do the experts predict?* [online]. eConsultancy. Available at: https://econsultancy.com/social -media-advertising-2023-trends-predictions/

7

Nature Is the Bottom Line

"Our age needs above all courageous hope and the impulse to creativeness."

—Bertrand Russell

JUST AS WE have both positive and negative forces impacting our lives and well-being, the same is true for nature. An executive director at the European Central Bank, Frank Elderson (2023), recently authored an opinion piece titled "The Economy and Banks Need Nature to Survive."

He wrote, "Humanity needs nature to survive, and so do the economy and banks. The more species become extinct, the less diverse are the ecosystems on which we rely. This presents a growing financial risk that cannot be ignored."

A growing number of banks and financial institutions are saying this.

Economies Need Nature to Survive

Elderson continues, "A thriving nature provides many benefits that sustain human well-being and the global economy. Think of fertile soils, pollination, timber, fishing stocks, clean water, and clean air. Unfortunately, intensive land use, climate change, pollution, over-exploitation, and other human pressures are rapidly degrading our natural resources. This nature loss poses a serious risk to humanity as it threatens vital areas, such as the supply of food and medicines. Such threats are also existential for the economy and the financial system, as our economy cannot exist without nature. Degradation of nature can impair production processes and consequently weaken the creditworthiness of many companies."

Nature isn't on the balance sheet, and it should be. It turns out that the European Central Bank looked at how dependent individual companies are on nature, and that dependency accounted for more than $4.5 trillion in loans. Stop for a minute to think about this. Companies are highly leveraged, banking on natural capital that is eroding. The stock market depends on nature, but we haven't priced that in. It's nuts. We are destroying nature and calling it GDP rather than calling this behavior what it is, a massive liability.

According to Elderson, 75% of European bank loans depend on nature.

I've seen this firsthand in the food industry, where droughts and flooding are causing companies to lose up to $50 million a year.

What we are talking about is scarcity. What happens if food companies, pharmaceutical companies, and others can no longer source the ingredients from nature that they need due to supply chain disruption caused by nature degradation? If supply chains are disrupted due to failing transportation vehicles, a company invests in new vehicles. So why aren't companies doing the same for our natural resources? It begs the question, again, why are we funding the destruction of nature through subsidies? And how can companies address this?

One of the concepts that Jessica Yellin of CNN shared (in Chapter 6) is "tikkun olam." It means "to heal the world." It is the concept of regeneration, one with deep roots in our agricultural and food systems.

So how do we bring this concept and value forward and integrate it into business?

Nature loss can amplify the transition risks of banks and their borrowers. Governments are increasing their efforts to protect the environment: the UN Convention on Biological Diversity set global targets in 2022, including the conservation of at least 30% of the world's lands, inland waters, coastal areas, and oceans. Efforts like this can lead to changes in regulation and policy, limiting the exploitation of natural resources or banning certain products that trigger degradation. Technological innovation, new business models, and changes in consumer or investor sentiment could also lead to transition risks and transition costs as companies are forced to adapt. Some older business models could disappear, while others might become too expensive and lose market share.

In a landmark study, according to the European Central Bank, De Nederlandsche Bank found that Dutch financial institutions alone have more than $500 billion in exposures to biodiversity risks. In a similar study, the Banque de France found that 42% of the value of securities portfolios held by French financial institutions consists of securities issued by companies dependent on at least one ecosystem service.

Early last year, the Central Banks and Supervisors Network for Greening the Financial System (NGFS) acknowledged that nature-related financial risk should be considered by central banks and supervisors in the fulfillment of their mandates.

And Kris Atkinson, portfolio manager; Ana Victoria Quaas, investment director; and Charlotte Apps, sustainable investing analyst, discuss the importance of biodiversity for bond investors and how debt markets can aim to effect real-world change on biodiversity. They stated in a new report by Fidelity (2023) called *Sleeping Giant*:

> While climate change is undoubtedly one of the most significant risks to the long-term profitability and sustainability of companies, biodiversity loss is an equally pressing issue that investors cannot ignore.

In the United States, the Inflation Reduction Act aims to support companies that are focused on regenerative business models, but as long as billions in subsidies continue to fund degenerative models, we're going to have a problem. Just as you can't outrun a bad diet, you can't out run $7.3 trillion in harmful subsidies.

Biodiversity loss refers to the gradual reduction in the variety and abundance of life on earth. Remember, biodiversity loss is driven by five key factors: land and sea use change, pollution, over-exploitation, climate change, and invasive species. All of this natural capital together provides what are called ecosystem services, such as pollination and food production, air circulation, climate regulation, flood protection, and carbon sequestration. We derive social, economic, and cultural benefits from these services.

To date, most investors have had carbon tunnel vision, focused almost exclusively on carbon. It is one indicator of biodiversity, but to ignore the other components puts everything at risk. The myopia is yet another blind spot. Water security is national security, and what we do to the soil, we do to our future. Investors must understand that natural capital is a vital asset for the functioning of the global economy and the material financial risks associated with its decline. It is estimated that more than 50% of global GDP is moderately or highly dependent on nature. The *Global Risks Report 2023* by the World Economic Forum has ranked "biodiversity loss" among the top five "risks that may have the most severe impact over the next 10 years."

Why are investors increasingly concerned? I wish it was simply because of these facts and the environmental destruction happening. But there is something else going on here, a not so invisible hand.

It is impacting costs, like insurance costs and the bottom line. Insurance is a key component to any business model. And if you look at what's happening in the insurance space when it comes to climate issues, it's pretty telling.

As biodiversity collapses, insurance costs are exploding, and insurance companies are pulling out of risky markets.

Insurance companies are a judge when it comes to determining the impact of climate. Because, if insurance companies won't insure homes in fire prone, hurricane prone, coastal erosion, and flood prone areas, it becomes an economic and financial discussion. And money talks.

Insuring Your Model

Wind, fire, and flood insurance are increasingly hard to get, especially in flood prone areas like Florida and California. The state of Florida now has to write insurance policies because the big insurance companies won't do it any longer, according to Monica Medina (2023), a former National Oceanic and Atmospheric Administration official. The ocean is absorbing 90% of the extra greenhouse gases, and that heat is trapping in not only the soil, but also the oceans. As water expands due to rising temperatures, coastal cities are at higher risk of flooding.

Global insured losses from natural disasters topped $130 billion in 2022, according to international risk management firm Aon (2023). "Insurance companies have regulated pricing in most states—they can't just charge consumers whatever they want," said

George Hosfield, senior director and general manager of home insurance solutions at LexisNexis Risk Solutions (AON, n.d.). But they can decide to pull out of a market if the economics no longer work, a tactic some insurers have exercised.

"Beyond California and Florida, states where consumers could see the most weather-related impact on coverage options or pricing include Arkansas, Louisiana, Nebraska, Iowa, Kansas, Oklahoma, Illinois, Kentucky, and Tennessee," said Stephen Bennett, chief climate officer at The Demex Group, which provides climate risk management solutions (AON, n.d.). That's America's heartland where farmers live and produce our food.

We can't just sell consumers climate smart products; we have to build these values into business. And that starts with where you set up headquarters and supply chain, to the homeowners insurance your employees can secure. All of these decisions impact your bottom line, employee retention, and costs.

Not to mention, they help to reduce volatility and mitigate costs in the long term (again, the fiduciary duty).

As Jacob Bogage (2023) reported in the *Washington Post*, "At least five large U.S. property insurers—including Allstate, American Family, Nationwide, Erie Insurance Group, and Berkshire Hathaway—have told regulators that extreme weather patterns caused by climate change have led them to stop writing coverages in some regions, exclude protections from various weather events and raise monthly premiums and deductibles."

The Impact of Climate Change on Your Bottom Line

Remember how 94% of the companies in the S&P cited their concern with climate risk? Insurance companies are confirming it. U.S. insurers have disbursed $295.8 billion in natural disaster claims over the past three years, according to international risk management firm Aon (2023). That's a record for a three-year period, according to the American Property Casualty Insurance Association (AON, n.d.). Natural catastrophes in the first six months of 2023 year in the United States caused $40 billion in insured losses, the third costliest first-half on record, Aon found.

"There's no place to hide from these severe natural disasters," said David Sampson, president of the American Property Casualty Insurance Association. "They're happening all over the country and so insurers are having to relook at their risk concentration."

In the agricultural industry, crop insurance is tied to on-farm practices that may actually be hindering the adoption of farming practices that help with water conservation and ecosystem management. Insurance companies play an important role here, and according Grey Moran (2023), "The Federal Crop Insurance Program helps steer the direction of U.S. agriculture. But advocates and farmers say its policies have often failed to benefit the most climate-adaptive farms—and penalizes farmers for adopting some climate-friendly strategies." It's another invisible hand.

Where you establish your company's headquarters has always mattered, affecting cost of living expenses, state taxes, and other costs. Now, you should consider the insurability of the region. We need to get smarter and build better. It is why we see the food industry exploring regenerative agriculture. Again, break down the word "regeneration" to its core "re-generation." To rebuild and renew for the next generation. What has been in place? The opposite: degenerative agriculture—systems that have been so damaging to natural resources and so extractive to assets like clean air, clean water, healthy soil that it is becoming criminal to continue this abuse.

Thankfully, companies like Lloyd's are warning insurers that more climate-related pain is to come, according to the *Financial Times* (Smith, 2023). Smith wrote about executives at Lloyd's calling for urgent investments in risk modeling: "Lloyd's of London has warned insurers that the full impact of climate change has yet to translate into claims data despite annual natural catastrophe losses borne by the sector topping $100bn. Insurance prices are surging as companies look to repair their margins after years of significant losses from severe weather to insured properties, exacerbated by inflation in rebuild costs. A warming planet has been identified by insurance experts and campaigners alike as a key factor." And that's not the end of it, according to Smith, "The prices charged by reinsurers, who share losses with primary insurers, rose by as much as 200% in January."

Our economy relies on nature. Destroying nature means destroying the economy. The best way to insure a business? Protect the resources on which it depends.

We have been killing the planet and calling it "GDP." And we can't insure our way out of it.

Our exposure to nature is massive and underrepresented on balance sheets. It impacts our employees with the escalating costs of homeowners and property insurance, and it impacts our bottom line, with the supply chain disruptions and more.

According to a paper by Hunter Lovins (2023), "There is a difference between extractive business models that benefit only a few parties, and those that deliver Regenerative Value Creation, increasing financial, shareholder, and stakeholder value by implementing practices that are both more profitable and more responsible to people and to the planet. These approaches cut costs, reduce risk, and make the company a more attractive partner for investors, customers, employees, and the whole of society. They enable a company to prosper by achieving an integrated bottom line."

So what does that look like? CDP's "Climate Action and Profitability" study shows that companies that manage their carbon emissions and mitigate climate change enjoy 18% higher returns on their investment than companies that don't and 67% higher returns than companies which refuse to disclose their emissions. Read those numbers again. This is good for your bottom line.

As explained in Chapter 1, ESG stands for "environmental, social and governance." Investors are increasingly applying these nonfinancial factors as part of their analysis process to identify material risks and growth opportunities.

And it's a hotbed of an issue in our polarized world. So let's step back from the label for a minute and think about the values here.

Is it the fiduciary duty of an executive to manage a company's risk? Yes, it is. Do the increasing number of storms, floods, fires, and other natural disasters present a growing financial risk to companies? Yes. Is it an executive's fiduciary duty to understand the marketplace and the changing social environment? Yes.

And is a company judged on its governance? Again, yes. And if nature has taught us anything it is that homogeneous systems fail. And right now, from the finance sector to venture capital funding, we have inherited capital markets that are largely homogenous. A Boston Consulting Group study of 1,700 companies in eight countries found that companies with above-average total diversity had both 19% higher innovation revenues and 9% higher EBIT margins, on average. Diversity is good for your bottom line (Lovins, 2023).

We do not have the same lived experiences, and bringing that diversity to leadership and decision-making is a revenue driver and a strength. There are 107 Historically Black Colleges and Universities (HBCUs) from which companies can recruit. Instead of labeling this as a "movement," perhaps it's better to focus on what it actually is: a fiduciary duty. At what point is the board held accountable for failing in its fiduciary duty to shareholders, given this data on diversity and biodiversity?

Biodiversity is necessary for resiliency, and yet, almost a third of the companies in the S&P 100 still lobby against measures to protect it. At what point will this become a class action lawsuit?

It's time to embed these values into business, as fundamental to the bottom line.

Another Ashley Madison Moment

One way to address the challenges facing 21st century businesses is through the regulatory system, and California is one example of that:

> New California law would force firms to report diversity metrics . . . . The bill requires venture capital firms operating in California to report the diversity breakdown of the founders they fund to the state; this includes reporting on the gender and ethnic and racial background of the founders, in addition to the dollar amount given to them . . . Supporters of the bill see it as a massive step toward increasing transparency in the venture capital industry, where less than 3% of all capital is allocated to women and Black founders. SB 54 would also require firms to collect and release their diversity data to the public. (Davis, 2023)

And for those wanting to label this is a fringe movement, Jamie Dimon, the CEO of JP Morgan, recently talked DEI metrics and how his firm recruits from HBCUs, with Fortune. Are they perfect? Not at all. Are they aware of the impact? Absolutely. Source https://finance .yahoo.com/news/jpmorgan-jamie-dimon-talks-dei-132700973 .html?guccounter=1&guce_referrer=aHR0cHM6Ly93d3cuZ29vZ2x lLmNvbS8&guce_referrer_sig=AQAAAArGQBn0ylET f9Q1L47C6W-miCfVFvWowndNr7D4vl_kE3QFgjDwc QkgrBKrFCOgXvUMtasq53yxv_frWVXSFFtb_RyQzvouZnd _Ni09H6LE1vkvYbOSIsX09RJgofd-V7vQgWU9W1w0oKL8_o _lUhWj5HpLGRIa14U340b0ak_Y. Another is the Taskforce for Nature Related Financial Disclosures (TNFD), a nature-related risk and opportunity management disclosure. Just as we have generally accepted accounting principles (GAAP), we will have generally accepted environmental principles, as investors increasingly realize the importance of natural assets. Legislation is already drafted.

Sustainability has been embedded in Japanese culture since the Edo period when resources were scarce (Christina, 2022), and I was fortunate to experience this firsthand, when my team at rePlant Capital engaged with leaders from Mitsui, a large Japanese keiretsu. The Mitsui team was exploring partnerships in the food industry that assisted in their goals to advance regenerative agriculture and smarter on farm practices for water conservation, carbon capture, and soil and topsoil preservation and stewardship.

But it goes beyond that today. Mark Minevich (2023) wrote in *Forbes*, "Japan, with its deep-rooted traditions and profound reverence for nature, has established itself as a frontrunner in the realm of green IT and AI solutions. Guided by the wisdom encapsulated in the famed Japanese proverb, 'The bamboo that bends is stronger than the oak that resists,' Japan has exhibited extraordinary resilience and adaptability in its fight against climate change. By pledging $36.8 million to support the 'Green Transformation' in four Pacific Island nations, Japan has demonstrated its commitment to driving environmental change and leading the global transition toward a sustainable future."

As businesses worldwide grapple with the imperative for environmental responsibility, Green IT and AI solutions have emerged as critical enablers in driving this transition. It's not just in Japan but across industries around the world. The team at AlphaCor Ltd, led by Chris Patton and a group of aerospace engineers and scientists, is revolutionizing energy, with thermodynamic experts converting heat to power, sub-zero power specialists refining cold energy breakthroughs, and thought-leaders building disruptive engineering solutions, because extinction is not an option. The caution, however—from industry experts and whistleblowers—over AI's lack of transparency, biases, discrimination, and ethical concerns need to be heeded, or we run the very real risk of codifying the discriminatory, homogenous, extractive systems that created extractive capitalism.

According to Minevich, "Green IT encompasses technologies and strategies that reduce the environmental impact of information technology, driving efficiency, cost savings, and innovation while helping organizations reduce their carbon footprint. By adopting these technologies and practices, organizations can optimize their energy usage, reduce waste, and minimize operational environmental impact. AI-powered Green IT solutions can enhance supply chain sustainability by optimizing transportation routes, minimizing fuel consumption, and promoting the use of eco-friendly vehicles. Moreover, implementing digital platforms to track and monitor the environmental impact of products throughout their life cycle helps businesses make more informed decisions and implement more sustainable practices."

For those starting companies, rather than creating the need to implement changes down the road, these systems can be integrated from the start. There is an opportunity in every sector and every category, from electric cars to AI. In 2019, Michelle Pfeiffer launched Henry Rose, a line of fine fragrances with not only deeply personal and sentimental scents, but an emphasis on transparency and strict standards for the healthiest ingredients. She now serves on the board of the Environmental Working Group, a nonprofit that got behind my work early. Everything we touch presents an opportunity. The demand for transparency across industries is only escalating, as human and planet health crises continue.

There also is a growing demand for accountability with voices like Meredith Whittaker's, who is the president of the Signal Foundation and current chief advisor, and the former faculty director and cofounder of the AI Now Institute, an American research institute studying the social implications of artificial intelligence and policy research that addresses the concentration of power in the tech industry. She's not alone.

Accountability is coming. More and more companies are stepping toward transparency. If transparency is bad for your business model, you may want to rethink your business model. Data are increasingly accessible and will be revealed across all sectors. In the food industry, companies like How Good ask simple questions of the cell-based meat companies like: What is the ratio of input to output? How many kilograms of feedstock (usually sugars, usually genetically engineered, always industrial) do you put into get one kilogram of finished product out? Approximately how much energy is required (in kilojoules or megajoules) to produce one kilogram of finished product? How Good is an independent research company and SaaS data platform with the world's largest database on food product sustainability. They provide real-time understanding and insight into a company's social and ecological impact. Again, if this kind of transparency is bad for your business model, you need a stronger business model.

Remember a few years ago when the list of clients who used Ashley Madison's website (the online dating service specializing in clandestine affairs) was leaked? In August 2015, a hacking group leaked more than 25 gigabytes of Ashley Madison data, including user details. It changed lives and careers. Industries will have their Ashley Madison moments, when what is invisible to the public becomes visible. If you are in a position where that kind of exposure makes you uncomfortable, get to work on what you need to change in your business model in order to be proud of your actions and to provide transparency to your customers. The best advice I got very early in my career is to never do anything you wouldn't want to read about on the front page of the *Wall Street Journal*. Your opposition and haters will target you. Make sure you can stand behind every action.

Light It Up

China is the leader in renewable energy installations, with a capacity of around 1,161 gigawatts, almost four times the United States, which is in second place, with a capacity of around 352 gigawatts (Jaganmohan, 2021). Stop for a minute and look at that differential. There is clearly a huge opportunity to invent, intervene, and innovate here.

Various types of renewable energy sources are used globally, including bioenergy, solar energy, hydropower, and geothermal energy, to name a few. According to Science Facts (2019), "Renewable energy is obtained from renewable natural resources (replenished naturally in a span of human life cycle). They are also referred to as clean energy as they do not contribute to carbon emissions, which makes them non-polluting."

So why switch? Well, Science Facts goes on to say: "Fossil fuels cause carbon-dioxide emission which is leading to global warming. In contrast, renewable energy sources are low cost, abundant and inexhaustible sources of energy and do not contribute to greenhouse gas emission."

In other words, it's not just an altruistic, planet-saving, tree-hugging thing. It actually is a global security, national security issue. Why build our energy supply on limited resources when renewable, naturally replenishable resources exist? Why risk geopolitical uncertainty and scarcity when solar, hydropower, and geothermal energy exist? Isn't it a board's fiduciary duty to mitigate risk? And as the World Bank highlighted, plenty of resources are available, more than $7 trillion in subsidies. Shouldn't we be reallocating them?

Biodiversity impacts fuel, food, fashion, fiber, water, and so much more. If you eat, drink, or clothe yourself, you depend on biodiversity every day. The investments in renewable energy infrastructure boost the economy of states and create new job opportunities for youth. In other words, that GDP counting that gets done and measured, this goes in the regenerative GDP column. An oil spill is going to pollute the Gulf of Mexico (or wherever it happens next); you don't have to worry about environmental pollution from a "solar spill." Some of these solutions are cost-effective, and some require sizable investments and/or a shift in the trillions of dollars of subsidies.

Globally, China and Canada are the top two countries in terms of generating the most energy through hydropower. Geothermal energy has been on the rise as well. Data show an increase in geothermal energy capacity globally in the last 10 years. Likewise, there has been a dramatic increase in the capacity of global solar energy in recent years.

And on farms, we see the introduction of tools like agro-voltaics. Lukas Walton at Builders Vision is active in this space, as is my friend Nicole Poindexter. Poindexter is the founder of Energicity, a leading off-grid, mini-grid developer in West Africa. Prior to founding Energicity, Poindexter was senior director global business development from startup to IPO in 2014 in leading the smart grid and utility software company Opower/Oracle. As if that wasn't enough, in 2011 Poindexter was appointed to be an inaugural member of the U.S. Department of Commerce Renewable Energy and Energy Efficiency Advisory Committee. Earlier in her career, Poindexter was senior policy advisor for the mayor's office in New York under the Bloomberg administration. She led economic development in Harlem and the Bronx, and she started several for-profit and not-for-profit organizations. She also happens to be a friend and former teammate of mine from high school. Founded in 2015, her company provides affordable, reliable, scalable electricity to 15 rural communities in Ghana and was the winner of a contract to serve an additional 32 communities in Sierra Leone.

In a profile piece, Joe Mandato (2019) wrote, "Nicole is a rare breed of innovator. She has the experience, vision, team, and products to solve one of the world's most vexing problems—first-time access to electricity for 1 billion people."

We've had a lot of back and forth, with her telling me that I need to get to the farms in Africa, and of me telling her that she needs to bring her model to the farms in the United States (both are true). And when she speaks about innovation in Ghana, she shares, "Businesses here are about innovations like how to deliver water. These businesses are immediately and very clearly improving people's lives. It inspires me to remember that innovation is best when it is fundamentally about building businesses that matter to the improvement of people's lives in very meaningful ways."

And her advice for American entrepreneurs? Listen.

When I asked her what role faith played in her work, she got quiet and said, "Are you writing about that?" Yes, I said. "I'm glad you told me, I will send you a link."

In that link, she shares how in the transition period between jobs, when she was deciding what to do after the public success of her prior company, that she read an article about the lack of electricity in Africa and felt that would be an interesting problem to solve. So she prayed a lot, and she read the entire Bible in one month. "After that, I just felt really grounded in God's promises," she shares. So she showed up in Africa and said, "I want to bring light." She comes from a place of complete calm when she speaks to it, a knowing of what she can do, and as she shares, a knowing "that God finishes what He starts."

Faith's Fuel

Why do I share this? Faith is going to play a role in your work, in whatever form that looks like for you. For some, it is deeply spiritual, like my friend Mark Eckhart, founder of One Million Truths, who practices Zen Buddhism. One Million Truths (OMT) is the first-ever platform dedicated to enabling solutions to resolve racial conflict by leveraging the power of AI. For others, like Poindexter, it is getting really quiet and leaning into prayer and scripture.

We often see athletes speak of faith and values. We see athletic coaches speak about it. We see it less often in business, yet when asked, most entrepreneurs will speak candidly about their faith and the practices they have in place. I would not have survived in my career or life without a deep, unwavering faith. The shape of that practice evolved and changed as I changed, from a commitment to church on Sunday mornings to what is now a daily prayer practice and meditation. Just like food is not one size fits all, faith is a spiritual nourishment, and it also is not one size fits all. Find what works for you, where you can connect to a source and power that is greater than you. For some it is God, for others, it is Nature, for others, it's the Universe or meditation, and for others, it may be another practice. Faith can be a powerful ingredient to your success.

Which reminds me of the words of Jay Shetty, a former monk who helps people rediscover their purpose: "Giving yourself space and time can actually lead to the birth of more creativity, better creativity, and some of your best work."

For me, that space and time comes from meditation and from running. There have been so many times when I have come in from a run and gone straight to my laptop or a notebook because so much has come in, in what feels like a download, during a run. I have learned to have a notepad and pen everywhere—in my car, in my bag—as I never know when something is going to come through, and I want to capture it when it does.

Permission to Pause

My friend with an M.D., Aviva Romm, calls this space and time "permission to pause." Whether that's in prayers, reading, meditation, or some other form of solitude, it's an important skill to be able to give yourself the space and time to center, ground yourself, and think.

Does a spiritual practice or a religious practice support an entrepreneur, especially when things get tough? Again, this is not meant to be a prescription but an offering, and for so many, the answer is yes.

So if faith helps insure a resiliency and strength in an entrepreneur, does it also provide some sort of inspiration?

The Romans believed that all people had a guiding spirit that attended them throughout their lives. Because this spirit was born with the person, it was called a "genius" (from the Latin verb *gignere* meaning "to give birth or bring forth"—which also happens to be the root of our word "generate"). A person's genius dictated their unique personality and disposition. If a person had an outstanding talent or ability, it was believed that this was due to their genius. From here it was a natural step for the word genius to be used not only of the spirit that inspired a talent but also of the talent itself.

The bottom line is that you have to make the space for creativity, genius, and inspiration. Oftentimes, a spiritual or meditative practice creates exactly that. As science continues to emerge on neuroplasticity of the brain, these spiritual practices serve as an additional tool to expand our imagination and creativity.

Action Steps: Healthy Practice Inventory

What supports you? Who supports you? Draft that list here. Is it a person, people, a team, a sister, or a friend who is like a sister? Is it triathlon training, a yoga practice, meditation, prayer, or church? Name it, list it, and lean into these practices and people. They are your supportive scaffolding; they are your strength when times get hard. Ask the people who you really respect if they have a spiritual or faith-based practice. While we often see athletes speaking about this, it's less likely that we see business leaders doing the same. But you may be surprised by what you learn.

Resources

AON. (n.d.). *United States insurance losses* [graph]. Available at: https://www.aon.com/reinsurance/catastropheinsight/global-regional-losses.html?region=United%20States&type=insured [Accessed 28 Nov. 2023].

Bogage, J. (2023, Sept. 3). Home insurers cut natural disasters from policies as climate risks grow. *Washington Post* [online]. Available at: https://www.washingtonpost.com/business/2023/09/03/natural-disaster-climate-insurance/

Christina. (2022). *Understanding sustainability in Japan and its role in travel* [online]. Arigato Travel. Available at: https://arigatojapan.co.jp/understanding-sustainability-in-japan-and-its-role-in-travel/

Collins Dictionary. (2016). *We take a look at the etymology behind the word "genius"* [online]. Collins Dictionary Language Blog. Available at: https://blog.collinsdictionary.com/language-lovers/we-take-a-look-at-the-etymology-behind-the-word-genius/

Davis, D.-M. (2023). *New California law would force firms to report diversity metrics* [online]. TechCrunch. Available at: https://techcrunch.com/2023/09/08/california-sb54-bill-diversity-venture/

Elderson, F. (2023). *The economy and banks need nature to survive* [online]. European Central Bank. Available at: https://www.ecb.europa.eu/press/blog/date/2023/html/ecb.blog230608~5cffb7c349.en.html

Fidelity International. (2023). *Sleeping giant: Bond markets are critical in the fight against biodiversity loss* [online]. Available at: https://s3-eu-west-1.amazonaws.com/germanfrontdoorv4prod-live-1324fb6294be47ceb7851ec22521-174be63/Germany%20PI/Pdf%20documents/sleeping-giant-biodiversity.pdf

Jaganmohan, M. (2021). *Renewable energy capacity worldwide by country 2019* [online]. Statista. Available at: https://www.statista.com/statistics/267233/renewable-energy-capacity-worldwide-by-country/

Lovins, H. (2023). *Integrated bottom line: A tool to quantify sustainable business performance* [online]. Available at: https://giteximpact.com/2023/05/25/integrated-bottom-line-a-tool-to-quantify-sustainable-business-performance/

Mandato, J. (2019). *Power player in West Africa* [online]. Medium. Available at: https://medium.com/joes-musings/power-player-in-west-africa-6b4272780ead

Medina, M. (2023). *"Insurance companies know": More people vulnerable as cost of climate disasters rises* [video]. YouTube. Available at: https://www.youtube.com/watch?v=FK_rXVIKArM

Minevich, M. (2023). Japan's green IT: A game changer in environmental sustainability. *Forbes* [online]. Available at: https://www.forbes.com/sites/markminevich/2023/07/18/japans-green-it-a-game-changer-in-environmental-sustainability/?sh=57085b9977d7

Moran, G. (2023). *How crop insurance prevents some farmers from adapting to climate change* [online]. Civil Eats. Available at: https://civileats.com/2023/09/20/how-crop-insurance-prevents-some-farmers-from-adapting-to-climate-change/

Science Facts. (2019). *Types of renewable energy: Sources, advantages & disadvantages* [online]. Available at: https://www.sciencefacts.net/types-of-renewable-energy.html

World Economic Forum. (2023). *WEF global risks report 2023* [online]. Available at: https://www.slideshare.net/wyakab/wef-global-risks-report-2023

8

How to Handle the Curveballs

"For those who thought they were putting water on my fire, you were really adding gas to it."

—Coco Gauff

WHEN I SPOKE with Nicole Poindexter about her work building Energicity and the challenges she faced, she shared how condescending people can be and offered, "You are leant wings by the storm." Resistance builds strength. Connie Schwartz-Morini, who works with Deion Sanders, Snoop Dog, and others says, "The more people who tell us why we can't do something just puts the battery in our back of why we can do it" (Feldman, 2023).

It's true that strength and determination are developed during some of our hardest times. And challenges are part of the human experience, especially in business. Rarely does anything go as planned. You may find yourself in situations where you have to downsize your team. You may find yourself in a legal situation in which you are dealing with an unethical attorney. Hard times are inevitable. I learned early in my career to not fight pain but to feel it in order to understand what lesson I was meant to learn from it. If putting yourself out there is hard, ask yourself why. If saying "no" is tough, get to the bottom of why and behaviors you may have learned when you were younger. If setting boundaries is difficult, explore your people-pleasing tendencies and where you first started behaving this way. If fundraising is hard, what lesson can you learn? If a team is in conflict, what can this teach you? Identify your patterns when times are tough, then question them. Some you'll want to keep; others you will want to change.

It helps to have good friends around you when this is happening because not only can they serve as a sounding board, but they can also encourage you to keep going. It gets back to that supportive scaffolding.

The word encouragement has the word "courage" tucked into it, hiding in plain sight: En-courage-ment.

To give another courage.

Some, like Sara Blakely, the founder of Spanx, routinely return to the teachings of someone like Wayne Dyer. Nicole Poindexter of Energicity sets boundaries, leans into her value system, her circle of influence, those who are very close in and honest, and she makes time to pray. To look at the incredible success of Sara Blakely and Spanx, you'd be hard-pressed to imagine that there were any naysayers. There were plenty, and having that supportive scaffolding is critical. The ones who keep your head up when things are looking down. Because when you're empty, it's impossible to pour yourself into something else. You want people around you who have your back.

Learning to ask for help isn't listed as a leadership skill, but it should be. That kind of self-awareness and vulnerability is absolutely in the best interest of a company.

Pain is part of the process, especially for an entrepreneur. There are moments when you feel like you've had the wind knocked out of you, and you find yourself on your knees because the load can be so heavy and hard. I've learned to view those moments of pain, even some of the most horrific pain, as a compass because they have led me to the most prosperous relationships and opportunities. They have forced me to open to support. Those moments directed me toward those who can help address the discomfort of the current situation and move into a new reality. It is really hard though, and it's often said that the universe will keep handing you the same situation in varying and increasingly aggressive forms until you figure it out.

If you ask any successful leader or entrepreneur, they will tell you that pain was part of the process. The discomfort helped them figure stuff out.

In my opinion, this is not talked about enough. Success is not a straight line. Along with the rejections, the nos, the naysayers, and the nonbelievers comes pain. And it's in those moments when you ask yourself, "Is this how I want my story to end? Is this the story I want to tell?" And if it's not, if you have a bigger dream or vision or hope for yourself, for your children, do all you can to figure out how to move through the discomfort and pain. You can't circumvent it. The path is straight through.

Which is why, in the last chapter of this book, I focus on your personal sustainability plan and the mental, physical, emotional, and spiritual health for business leaders. Because more often than not, when we see someone destroy something they've created, it's because they developed unhealthy coping mechanisms or addictions to deal with the discomfort.

You can't run from yourself. You can try to numb pain with all kinds of things, substances, and new people, but if you're not happy with yourself, by yourself, it eventually reveals itself.

Building Your Resiliency

That is why the theme of courage is so important to me in driving change in business, especially as it relates to entrepreneurship. Brené Brown shares in her now famous TED Talk that the root of the word courage is cor—the Latin word for heart. In one of its earliest forms, the word courage meant "to speak one's mind by telling all one's heart." In the French language, *coeur* is the word for heart. Courage to speak one's mind, to live one's truth, to tell one's story is so much easier when done from the heart. Our minds can be fickle; our hearts know the truth. And to live in that truth as an entrepreneur is incredibly brave work. It does not take much to have a new idea; we all have them dozens of times in a day! It does take a lot to act on it, to be brave enough to share it with someone, to power through self-doubt, the what-ifs, the naysayers, the "what will people say?" and to move consciously through the discomfort and uncertainty into bringing a new idea into the world.

If I'd stopped and listened to all of the naysayers when I first began this work on cleaning up our food system, I never would have done it. When I shared how polluted our food system had become and how our food companies had a double standard, producing the same products in other countries with better ingredients, and people close to me suggested that I do nothing, I felt like I was being told not to breathe. Behind those comments were, "What can you do? What if you fail?" Sometimes directly, sometimes indirectly. If you look closely, the people saying those things is reflecting their experiences, their understanding, their skills, and their paradigm thinking and expectations. They're standing in their own shoes, not in yours. Only you know if you can do it. Only you know if you have the experience, the resiliency, the strength to see something through. You can reframe every setback as a lesson. And sometimes, those close to you are really comfortable with keeping you where you are. It may be an attempt at protection too, but an entrepreneur needs an inordinate amount of support, not resistance and negativity, from those closest to them. It's why your supportive scaffolding is so important.

So if you're encountering resistance, ask yourself, "Does this person want to hold me back? Do they want to maintain the status quo? Does this person feel the need to personally attack? Does this person need control? Does someone want you to stay small? And is there something else that can serve as a stronger support system?"

And what happens if I make this change? What happens if I allow myself to expand into all that I am meant to be, leaving the shackling beliefs, mindsets, and relationships behind?

Chances are, you really have no idea what happens when you make that change. But what you do know is what you're capable of. I call it your "figure-it-out" quotient, your *FQ*. Do you have the ability to figure something out? And do you have people around you that believe in you too? That believe in your ability to figure it out.

Because those are the people you want around you. The naysayers are a dime a dozen. They tend to care a lot about how your change is going to impact them. They will talk about you behind your back. But the ones who have your back, the ones who give support and say, "OK, I believe in you, to figure it out," those are your people. They are your supportive scaffolding. And they're critically important on this journey.

Handling Curveballs

I was very lucky in one of my first jobs during business school. I worked on the fixed income desk at AIM (now Invesco) for a woman named LuAnn Katz. At the time, I was dealing with someone who was proving to be incredibly difficult, and Katz shared something that stuck with me ever since: your happiness in life is determined by how you handle the curveballs. Some people will get more than their fair share of curveballs in life, but we all get them. And when we get thrown a curveball, how we choose to respond will define the next chapter. The word responsibility can be broken down to "response-ability" or "our ability to respond." More often than not, however, we react. So you have to slow the roll when something is happening, especially something hard, and think about how you want to respond and your ability to respond. Some of the biggest decisions I've made in my life took years. Give yourself that time and space to prepare.

So what makes it possible for some people to respond to curveballs in a way that up levels their life, while for others, a curveball seems to break it?

This is where someone's FQ comes in, their ability to figure it out. You have a choice with every curveball, to let it knock you down and stay there, or to get back up. If you've got a low FQ, it will keep you in victim mode. A higher FQ will inspire you out of it and into action. We all have bad things happen to us. Sometimes, horrific things happen to good people, and yet we watch people overcome incredible odds. Your FQ is determined by a host of factors. It's a function of several things, a formula that includes tenacity, optimism, honesty, community, creativity, curiosity, network, strength, resilience, open mindedness, mindset, beliefs, and more. It is not a simple formula, which is why individuals have a varying degrees of FQ.

I first began understanding the importance of FQ as a student in business school, when the absolute tsunami of work made it necessary to not only learn but also to prioritize and organize. I honed it on the trading desk in my first job out of business school, meeting management teams of thousands of companies, and meeting founders and executives from multinational corporations. And I will add, it is also developed further when I became mother of four. There is so much that you have to figure out when you have children and so many curveballs. Not surprisingly, successful companies have leaders with high FQs. An important part of developing your FQ is knowing when to ask for support.

When I was at an investor conference in Oakland about five years ago, a small group of women, four of us, got together for dinner in the hotel restaurant. All of us were mothers working in the food and finance industries. And as we put a cone of silence over that dinner table, we realized that we were all dealing with very similar issues at work. We weren't just colleagues; we were allies. Few, if any of us, had female mentors, and none of us had a safe place to recount our stories, flesh them out, and find a way to move certain issues forward. The next morning, when we shared it with another colleague, she christened the group with a name, and it changed everything. The five of us have held virtual monthly get-togethers ever since, juggling the demands of motherhood, work, the challenges encountered in the workplace, and we've shown up for each other through all kinds of career and life changes. That group has expanded so much that it is now a conference that I cofounded that supports women transforming the food and finance industries.

The greatest way you can support someone is to have their back. How you talk about them when they're not in the room is everything. How you share their name when there is opportunity. How you show up for them so that they feel seen and heard is game-changing. In the South (where I am originally from), there is a term for strong women who have each other's backs: Steel Magnolias. I think of it every time I support another strong woman or when a strong woman supports me. It is a beautiful, collective show of strength.

And as entrepreneurs, you really need this support system. It is supportive scaffolding that helps you grow into and reach your highest FQ, with the mentors, family, friends, and allies who help you figure it out.

Assembling Your Hype Squad

My friend Erin Gallagher does an amazing job at building this supportive scaffolding and community. She's founded countless organizations all with the shared goal to #HypeWomen. Her goal is to elevate the voices of women in business and leadership. She went viral when she wrote a LinkedIn post on her phone while waiting to meet a friend for lunch. What happened next sent shock waves through millions of women.

Gallagher shared in her post,

I couldn't stop thinking about the image of Jamie Lee Curtis at the Golden Globes hyping Michelle Yeoh for her historic Best Actress win for *Everything Everywhere All at Once*. We so rarely see a woman publicly celebrating another woman's success as if it's her own.

And when I can't stop thinking about something, I write. It's a frenetic energy that refuses to be silenced until it's released through prose out into the world. Imagine a toddler tugging at your shirt asking for attention until you kneel down, look into her eyes and say, "I see you."

The Unabashed Hype Woman "word anthem" (as described by JLC herself) halted the hustle and grind of our lives to look every woman in the eye and say, "I see you."

Within hours, the post went viral across multiple social media platforms. On LinkedIn, it almost immediately garnered 1.2M impressions; 22,000 reactions; 964 comments; and 2,284 reposts.

And as a PR person, being featured in the following publications without pitching doesn't happen every day or without an authenticity that is determined and driven by what resonates most.

Gallagher's post appeared on the *Today Show*, HuffPost, *People* magazine, the *Guardian*, Yahoo, Parade, *Los Angeles Times*, *Us Weekly*, *Daily Mail*, AsiaOne.com, and *Page Six/New York Post* and it was shared in the feeds of the Female Quotient, FEMINIST, George Takei, and GOOD Worldwide Inc.

But, by far, her favorite article covering the movement was written by Annie Reneau (2023), which starts, "De-condition and unlearn what you've been wired to think: that women are your competition." Because, as Gallagher shares, it focuses on the heart of the message: the seismic shift in the way women view one another and themselves.

"This is a *move*ment, not a moment," she writes.

In other words, don't let the existing paradigm blind you.

All too often, unfortunately, that is exactly what happens. People dismiss these emerging changes as trends or fads. To do so would be a grave mistake. Pain is an early leading indicator for change. Pain can serve as a powerful compass.

And the planet is clearly in pain.

Detoxing Your Capital

The World Bank recently issued a new report (2023) about the ways that current financial models and subsidies are destroying natural capital and our planet's resources. In the report, the authors wrote:

> Clean air, land, and oceans are critical for human health and nutrition and underpin much of the world's economy. Yet they suffer from degradation, poor management, and overuse due to government subsidies. "Detox Development: Repurposing Environmentally Harmful Subsidies" examines the impact of subsidies on these foundational natural assets. Explicit and implicit subsidies—estimated to exceed US$7 trillion per

year—not only promote inefficiencies but also cause much environmental harm. Poor air quality is responsible for approximately 1 in 5 deaths globally.

As the analyses in this report show, a significant number of these deaths can be attributed to fossil fuel subsidies, which means that we are actually subsidizing these deaths.

According to the World Bank, "Agriculture is the largest user of land worldwide, feeding the world and employing 1 billion people, including 78% of the world's poor. But it is subsidized in ways that promote inefficiency, inequity, and unsustainability. Subsidies are shown to drive the deterioration of water quality and increase water scarcity by incentivizing over extraction." The World Bank is telling us that we are subsidizing our own extinction.

Global direct government expenditures in the three sectors fossil fuels, agriculture, and fisheries are $1.25 trillion a year—around the size of the economy of Mexico (World Bank, 2023). To subsidize fossil fuel consumption, countries spend about six times what they pledged to mobilize annually under the Paris Agreement for renewable energies and low-carbon development.

In other words, when it comes to allocating capital toward these solutions, we're not walking the talk. Countries are spending six times more on degenerating the planet than on regenerating it. Countries are investing six times more on destructive practices than on constructive ones. Any second grader could do the math here. Because while governments talk about funding solutions and stopping environmental destruction, they are still subsidizing the industries doing it, spending six times more on the destruction of our natural resources than on solutions. No wonder people are starting to sue governments and companies. The practices that these companies are engaged in, leveraging these toxic subsidies, are patterns of addiction and abuse.

The Thumb on the Scale

If capital is the first ingredient in any company, then these subsidies should be viewed as the liabilities that they are, a thumb on the scale that gives an enormous financial advantage to those who receive them, while trashing the planet. All too often, capitalism is declared "ruthless," but it might be a better adjective for these subsidies.

According to the World Bank, subsidies "are responsible for 14% of annual deforestation, incentivizing the production of crops that are cultivated near forests. These subsidies are also implicated in the spread of zoonotic and vector-borne diseases, especially malaria. Finally, oceans support the world's fisheries and supply about three billion people with almost 20% of their protein intake from animals. Yet they are in a collective state of crisis, with more than 34% of fisheries overfished, exacerbated by open-access regimes and capacity-increasing subsidies."

The World Bank report fills significant knowledge gaps using new data and methods. In doing so, it enhances understanding of the scale and impact of subsidies and offers solutions to reform or repurpose them in efficient and equitable ways.

"People say that there isn't money for climate but there is—it's just in the wrong places," said Axel van Trotsenburg, senior managing director of the World Bank. "If we could repurpose the trillions of dollars being spent on wasteful subsidies and put these to better, greener uses, we could together address many of the planet's most pressing challenges."

The report notes that government subsidies of $577 billion in 2021 to artificially lower the price of polluting fuels, such as oil, gas, and coal, exacerbate climate change and cause toxic air pollution, inequality, inefficiency, and mounting debt burdens. Remember those Exxon scientists? They knew this too. Redirecting subsidies could unlock at least half a trillion dollars toward more productive and sustainable uses. So why aren't we doing this? Because the companies that are now addicted to these subsidies are acting like addicts, desperate for more.

Remember how 94% of companies in the S&P 100 know that climate change is impacting them, but a third of those companies are lobbying against policies that would protect them against climate change? These companies are displaying the tendencies of an addict. They know that these subsidies are toxic, yet they're addicted to them. According to the World Bank report, "In agriculture, direct subsidies of more than $635 billion a year are driving the excessive use of fertilizers that degrade soil and water and harm human health." We are literally trashing the planet and calling it "subsidies." It turns out that subsidies for products such as soybeans, palm oil, and beef push into the forests and are responsible for 14% of forest loss every year. Why does this matter? The forests are the lungs of the planet. The carbon dioxide that we breathe out, the forests breathe in. They are a critical part of the planet.

If we are not only subsidizing the destruction of planet health but also human health, isn't it time for reform? States are now suing the fossil fuel companies, and consumers are suing the agrochemical companies. Who wants to lead a business model with this type of liability? It's no wonder investors and asset managers are pushing for change. They are simply managing risk.

"With foresight and planning, repurposing subsidies can provide more resources to give people a better quality of life and to ensure a better future for our planet," said Richard Damania, chief economist of the Sustainable Development Practice Group at the World Bank. "Much is already known about best practices for subsidy reform, but implementing these practices is no easy feat due to entrenched interests, challenging political dynamics, and other barriers."

So why am I sharing this? Because asset managers are demanding change. Because any business model built on this foundation has a liability at its core.

Policy isn't someone else's problem. Policy is money, and these subsidies have the ability to either regenerate GDP or degenerate it. Policy can build healthy ecosystems or destroy them. That chief sustainability officer we talked about earlier? That person should be making sure that policy is changing to meet the changing needs of their twenty-first century consumers and investors.

We know how critical capital allocation is to building new businesses and industries, and subsidies and the policies driving them are the elephants in the room here. They are a country's values on clear display. If we're going to talk about collecting data on emissions and Scopes 1, 2, and 3, we should also calculate what some are now calling "Scope 0" and the amount of money spent lobbying to influence policy and subsidy expenditure. It's one of the earliest indicators of a company's intent and actions.

When the World Bank comes out with a report like this one, stating so clearly how these subsidies are polluting the planet and making us sick, it's on business to demand better. Otherwise, escalating pollution costs, impacting everything from supply chains, to water scarcity, to carbon and health will continue to impact your bottom line.

We share this one planet. If these subsidies are polluting the planet, destroying the ecosystem we all need to survive, we cannot afford to accept it as business as usual. We cannot outrun the data.

We have a choice: we can keep subsidizing the destruction or we can fund solutions.

We can build business models that don't pollute the planet, that don't rely on toxic subsidies, from people or government purses. And if you think about it, if you're in an industry that does rely on them, you'll spend a significant amount of money defending yourself rather than focusing on your core competency. It will become an ever larger, growing distraction. You can't be both anticipating the worst and creating the best, just like you can't frown and smile at the same time.

These toxic subsidies should really be viewed for what they are: detrimental to the bottom line of any business, even those receiving them. They are liabilities. And isn't it your fiduciary duty to mitigate risk? If the capital funding your business is destructive and toxic, any promises you are pedaling in the press are greenwashing.

If you're going to seed innovation, how and where you source capital matters.

Recovery from these business models isn't accomplished by fighting unhealthy old paradigms; it is accomplished by choosing to fund and create healthy, fair, and just ones. We are watching the real-time exploration of a new model in cryptocurrency, and my friend and business partner, Holly Ruxin of Montcalm TCR, talks about how important the right relationships are, not only with people, but also with money. She's been in impact and investments for her entire career, with most of her time spent at Morgan Stanley, outperforming just about everyone else.

In December 2022, we co-hosted a small convening together and invited friends to explore how they felt about their money, if it was invested in a way that is aligned with their values. It planted the seed of something so much bigger, and in November 2023, Montcalm TCR, Ruxin, myself and others hosted our first conference together at the Presidio Officer's Club.

Fifteen years ago, when I was calling for changing the food system, few were paying attention; most thought it naive. And they were wrong.

It's time to rethink the financial system, its extractive nature and externalized costs. There will be plenty who will say (again), "Good luck with that, Robyn." And I am reminded (again) of that Margaret Mead quote, like so many times before: "Never doubt that a small group of thoughtful committed individuals can change the world. In fact, it's the only thing that ever has."

Ruxin calls it the architecture of freedom. It's a perfect way to describe financial resiliency and health. We are so intentional about how we architect our diets, what we consume, what we put into our grocery carts. And yet, at the same time, we are surprisingly in the dark when it comes to the financial products we use. Just as we had to break up with food companies that weren't good for us, the same opportunity is presenting itself here, and a growing number of financial services firms, like Montcalm, are proving to be better-for-you, too.

Montcalm does a lot of work with bonds, impact bonds to be exact. Bonds are a way to preserve capital while investing, so Montcalm works with its investors who provide upfront funding to finance specific projects, and then its investors are repaid based on specified outcomes being achieved. Examples are social impact bonds, green bonds, and environmental bonds. In other words, its investors not only have a predictable income stream, but they also know exactly where their money is going, the impact it is making on issues that they care about, and what it is doing. Imagine if this was the status quo.

Do you know where your money sleeps at night? The savings you put into a bank are used by the bank. Do you know how? Do you know where that money goes? Is that bank lending to the fossil fuel industry? Is that bank funding the agricultural models you love or the ones you despise? How transparent is your financial institution? Are you invested in companies that align with how you grocery shop? We demand that transparency in almost every industry, especially food, so how can we get more transparent, more creative with capital? How can we create financial products that incorporate environmental and social metrics? Danone, a 100-old company that was certified as B Corp, in 2018 received a $2 billion loan with a striking condition: a lower interest rate only if Danone maintains its B Corp status, which I cover in the next chapter.

My friend Ellie Rubenstein, the founder of Manna Tree, built out a powerful and successful private equity firm that invests in better-for-you companies that support human health. It was born out of health crisis that she experienced. Rather than turn to others for a solution, she created one, building a private equity firm that invests in companies that are addressing our health crises. I often say, "You can't fix a broken food system with a broken financial system." Our financial system is highly extractive, and it externalizes costs. Ellie's firm is doing the exact opposite. Rather than using capital in an extractive manner, she is using it in a restorative and regenerative way. She's hired the very best, those with firsthand experience in the food system, like Steve Young, whom I worked with when General Mills acquired Annie's. He was inside of a multinational food company and saw how better-for-you food is a growing category. He now brings the operational experience learned at General Mills to scaling better-for-you products.

Can you imagine if the multinational banks did the same and created better-for-you financing for the food industry? Or if bonds were linked to outcomes like soil nutrient density? We might just be able to build a healthier food system, sickness and disease obsolete.

Who Sleeps with Your Capital?

We can create financial products that are "better-for-you" and better for the planet: Products that tie loan terms to the environment, equity, and impact metrics. Subsidies that regenerate biodiversity, benefiting the natural capital systems on which our economy depends. Just as we had to get really brave and admit that our food system wasn't good for us, the same is required here.

As Howard Collinge writes in *Beautiful Economics* (2015), "In our current economic model, humans are one-dimensional units in a giant mathematical equation. If the equation leads to bigger and bigger gross domestic product (GDP), higher share prices, and more cars, the economy is doing fine. The same economic model has produced ever widening inequalities, with 20% of the world now consuming 86% of its goods, while the poorest 20% consume 1% or less and emit 2% of the world's greenhouse gases. Something doesn't quite add up."

It doesn't add up. Your employees and consumers know it. When General Mills acquired Annie's, I was brought in by the Annie's team to help with the integration. My friend Steve Young, who now works with Rubenstein at Manna Tree, shared that one of the biggest benefits to General Mills in that acquisition was the retention of top talent and the ability to recruit top candidates from business schools. Why? Because it was suddenly very clear to everyone in the market that General Mills understood the value of better-for-you products. Actions always speak louder than words.

Another company that I worked with that transitioned not only their brand but also their product line was a surprising one, Isagenix. Isagenix was long known for its weight loss shakes and its network marketing. I was brought in to present to the board, offering insight on what the twenty-first century consumers are looking for: free-from, more plant-based options, and transparency. I shared the opportunity to expand the portfolio of products to reflect that. In that meeting, only a handful of board members were on board with the vision, and the majority were not, so nothing changed. They were dead set on their existing model, just like Blockbuster. The paradigm blindness was strong.

And then Sharron Walsh was promoted to CEO. Prior to joining Isagenix, she built one of the fastest-growing direct sales and marketing companies in her native country of Australia. And according to Charlie Katz (2021), "She excelled at assembling strong teams in the field and driving overall business growth and profitability."

She quickly restructured the company's portfolio of products, scaled the development of free-from offerings, and brought in an incredible Harvard-trained scientist named Dr. Plant to lead product development. Her mindset wasn't "either or" but "both and." The change is palpable. Perhaps the most telling quote from Katz's article is when Walsh states, "It's important to acknowledge that we don't know what we don't know and then establish programs where the voices of the employee body and customers can be heard." According to Katz, Walsh "established a diversity, equality, and inclusion collective made up of nine employees representing different ethnicities, races, genders, backgrounds, and other diverse attributes as well as an external consultant with experience in this area. This group meets monthly with the primary intent to listen to and learn from one another on how we can become better together so that everyone in Isagenix feels safe, included, and equal." Walsh listens and builds out areas of expertise, and she operates with honesty and transparency. She listens, and she took a brand at risk of obsolescence and revitalized it.

You have a company that was running the risk of obsolescence, largely known for work done in the twentieth century, now completely reformulating itself to meet the needs of not only twenty-first century consumers but also twenty-first century employees who are demanding flexible work options after experiencing fully remote work during COVID-19.

According to the *Wall Street Journal*, "At the start of the COVID-19 pandemic, women were pushed out of the workforce at an alarming rate, sparking a full-blown 'she-cession.'" There were dire predictions that it would take years to recover from the drop (Lipman, 2023).

The exact opposite happened. Post-pandemic, a record number of women are in the workplace. In June, 77.8% of women ages 25 to 54 were working or looking for jobs, up from 77.6% in May and the highest in U.S. history, the Labor Department's recent jobs report showed (Davidson, 2023).

The return to office mandates are a disaster for working mothers. The *Wall Street Journal* has an article with that exact title. Some companies, like Once Upon A Farm, co-founded by Cassandra Curtis, Ari Raz, John Foraker, and Jennifer Gardner, have fully embraced remote work.

According to Lipman (2023), "A global survey of CEOs found that almost two-thirds expect a full five-day-a-week return to the office by 2026." In the words of co-founder and CEO John Foraker, "Once Upon a Farm is committed to remaining a 'remote first' employer. Why? Simple. It's created a ridiculous unfair competitive advantage for us in securing and retaining talent top talent. We know because we've more than doubled headcount since early 2020, and we are able to hire the most incredible talent, no matter where they are. It's showing up clearly in our growth, creativity, ability to execute, and overall business results."

Remote work brought record numbers of women into the labor pool, bringing in more talent and more diversity.

Thankfully, more and more companies, from legacy brands to the cutting-edge companies building out AI platforms and Web3, are realizing that in order to capture market share and the next generation of employees, they have to be in sync with the changing needs of younger demographics. The number of choices for top talent are growing because a growing number of companies are realizing that the current look, of being narrow-minded, subsidy addicts and those who abuse the planet, isn't good for employee retention, customers, public relations, or their investors.

Bank on Change

One of the leading voices who has been saying this for a long time is my friend Kat Taylor, the founder of Beneficial State Bank. Taylor is an activist and philanthropist who has made it her life mission to bring equity to underserved and underrepresented communities across the country. She started a bank, a venture capital firm, and an agribusiness to use capitalism's toolbox to fight systemic racism, environmental destruction, and economic inequality.

According to Kristin Stoller (2020), "Way back in 2007 (the stone age in impact investing), Kat Taylor and Tom Steyer launched an idea they'd talked about for years: Use a charitable foundation to start a bank that would lend to nonprofits and do-gooder businesses and direct its profits back to their environmental and community charitable causes. With Taylor as CEO, Beneficial State Bank has grown into a $1.1 billion institution with 13 branches stretching from Washington to Southern California . . . . From the first, Taylor made sure that at least 75% of Beneficial's loans went to organizations promoting some mission (e.g., affordable housing, social justice, and environmental sustainability) or to businesses that were women- or minority-led."

Mark Watson, a friend of Taylor's, has seen it his entire career. Watson is cofounder and president of Potlikker Capital, a farm community-governed charitable integrated capital fund dedicated to supporting BIPOC farmers at the intersection of racial and climate justice. Potlikker Capital is a supporting entity to Jubilee Justice. Watson also serves as senior investment strategist after serving as managing director of the Fair Food Fund, which offers catalytic capital with a social equity lens to improve community access to healthy food and increase wealth through more local ownership of the means of the production and distribution of food.

Watson is also the founder of Keel Asset Management LLC, a financial advisory firm that provides socially responsible financial planning and investment advisory services to nonprofits and public and corporate pension plans.

According to Potlikker Capital's site, Watson started his career as a banker at the First National Bank of Chicago, now JP Morgan, in commercial banking and corporate and public finance. He had a

30-year career that included managing investment portfolios for foundations, endowments, and institutional pension funds. Most recently, Watson co-designed and launched an integrated racial justice capital fund, the Boston Impact Initiative Fund, and managed the deployment of capital to more than 30 small businesses. Watson continues as an investment committee member of the Boston Impact Initiative Fund; an advisory board member of MIT/Health Innovation Systems Inc.; director of transition of the Institute of Educational Leadership; board president of Sustainable Cape, Inc.; and a former board member of the Social Venture Network. Beneficial has made more than $700 million in loans, and Taylor is Beneficial's chair. His life's work has been to demonstrate a smarter, more inclusive model.

Because banks have limitations. Limitations that Watson knew. According to Taylor, "Beneficial had to turn down loan applications from a slew of promising entrepreneurs—many of them from BIPOCs (referring to Black, Indigenous and People of Color)—because their credit profiles were just too risky for a regulated and FDIC insured bank."

Which begs the question, how antiquated and discriminatory are those FDIC regulations? That question probably merits its own book.

That's when, because of those discriminatory regulations, Taylor started thinking about the need for an integrated impact capital strategy—including not just lending and philanthropy, but venture capital investing, too.

According to Stoller (2020),

"The systems that we are working in are complex with no one-size-fits-all solutions," Taylor says. "To gain freedom from the devastating Black-White dynamic, we will have to shift assets. Disinvested communities who have been hurt the worst may require grants to build capacity for capital absorption, but they also deserve productive equity capital for community development, control and ownership." In other words, those who have been historically discriminated against and denied a shot at realizing the capitalist dream, need to get one.

So Taylor started making a few venture capital investments through the foundation that owned Beneficial—for example, putting money into a Black-led clean energy fund. After becoming more familiar with and making contacts in the venture capital world, Taylor officially entered it. She pulled together a team of four partners, including herself, and put some $25 million into for-profit Radicle Impact."

"Just like the bank is trying to change the banking system for good, Radicle is trying to be a good venture firm with aligned values," she says.

Radicle has put over $45 million into 27 portfolio companies. More than half its portfolio companies have founders or CEOs who are women or people of color, compared to a third of all venture-capital backed companies, according to an analysis of Crunchbase data by the Kauffman Fellows Research Center.

"Ultimately, the real measure of society will be whether we need philanthropy at all," she declares. "It's kind of an admission of failure because if we were running society right, we wouldn't need to give people money." The question again becomes: Where can you be braver in your life?

Planned Obsolescence

This keeps coming up, to make the need for philanthropy or a chief sustainability officer or impact capital obsolete. It's the ultimate success of a movement, to make the need disappear. It's how I felt when I launched AllergyKids back in 2006. Very few were taking the food allergy space seriously, recognizing it for its unique needs and the enormous demographic it is. I drafted a business plan and the mission was "to create universal awareness of life-threatening food allergies" and wrote in it: my hope is to make this organization obsolete. Did AllergyKids do that on its own? Not at all, but a few years ago, I knew that we, and hundreds of other organizations and millions of families, had accomplished that mission.

What type of system needs to be in place so that philanthropy is obsolete? A system with justice and equity at its core, an inclusive one that addresses both human and environmental needs. It is a system that does not discriminate and recognizes that nothing is separate. We are waking up to how connected all of us are, to nature and each other, how rather than each being a single thread, we actually are woven together as one fabric. How we treat one demographic, one race, one gender, one ethnicity, impacts the weave of the entire fabric. If one thread starts to fray, the whole is compromised. Just as we've created "better-for-you" categories in the food industry, there is a huge opportunity to do the same in finance.

Action Steps: Description Inventory

Before you get going, let's take inventory. I want to help you define your FQ, so create a list of all of the adjectives that describe you. Make two columns. In one, note the adjectives you use to describe yourself, and in the other, note the ones that are often given to you ("passionate" is one I hear all the time!). I also want you to create another list, two columns again. In the first column, list the people you turn to for support, the ones who immediately come to mind who have your back. In the second column, list the ones who make you feel badly about yourself (the bullies, whether online or in real life).

And lastly, I want you to list out your unique skills, the things that you know you are really good at. Perhaps you're highly intuitive or amazing at tech or really good at branding. Hold on to these lists for now. There is a buoyancy to a high FQ that will serve you, power you, and fuel you through endeavors, and thankfully, it is something that can be developed, which is the goal here.

Resources

Bernard, D. (n.d.). Rise in CEOs linking pay to engagement and diversity targets. *HR Magazine* [online]. Available at: https://www.hrmagazine.co.uk/content/news/rise-in-ceos-linking-pay-to-engagement-and-diversity-targets/

Charlie Katz in an article for Medium called "Five Things I Wish Someone Told Me Before I Became CEO."

Collinge, H. (2015). *Beautiful economics: A guide to a gentle world domination.* Simon & Schuster.

Davidson, P. (2023). Post-pandemic, there's a record number of women in the workplace. Can the trend continue? *USA Today* [online]. Available at: https://www.usatoday.com/story/money/2023/07/11/women-at-work-record-level/70402718007/

Feldman, B. (2023). *Meet the woman behind Deion Sanders' "Coach Prime" business empire* [online]. Athletic. Available at: https://theathletic.com/4836011/2023/09/12/deion-sanders-manager-constance-schwartz-morini/

Katz, C. (2021). Sharron Walsh of Isagenix: Five things I wish someone told me before I became a CEO. *Medium* [online]. Available at: https://medium.com/authority-magazine/sharron-walsh-of-isagenix-five-things-i-wish-someone-told-me-before-i-became-a-ceo-41e955c4e8f

Lipman, J. (2023, Dec. 15). Return-to-office mandates are a disaster for working mothers. *Wall Street Journal.* Available at:

Reneau, A. (2023). *Thousands of women share image of Jamie Lee Curtis and Michelle Yeoh with a powerful message* [online]. Upworthy. Available at: https://www.upworthy.com/jamie-lee-curtis-michelle-yeoh-hype-women

Stoller, K. (2020). Meet billionaire politician Tom Steyer's wife, a pioneering impact investor on a mission to spend $1 billion righting society's wrongs. *Forbes* [online]. Available at: https://www.forbes.com/sites/kristinstoller/2020/10/09/meet-billionaire-politician-tom-steyers-wife-a-pioneering-impact-investor-on-a-mission-to-spend-1-billion-righting-societys-wrongs/?sh=1817e6bd1aae

World Bank. (2023). Trillions wasted on subsidies could help address climate change. *World Bank Report* [online]. Available at: https://www.worldbank.org/en/news/press-release/2023/06/15/trillions-wasted-on-subsidies-could-help-address-climate-change

9

Risk Mitigation and Transparency

"The way to get started is to quit talking and begin doing."

—Walt Disney

IF ALL OF us woven together create a fabric that we call "humanity," then all consumption put together is the thing we call "GDP."

But as we've already discussed, GDP does not distinguish between good or bad consumption or take into consideration the long-term consequences of toxic subsidies, externalized costs, and environmental damage. So is it the best metric for tracking what companies are doing to the planet—if they're boosting GDP but destroying the resources we need to survive?

GDP, as we currently measure it, doesn't care. A business can trash the planet and boost GDP. A business can make families sick with polluted water and boost GDP. A business can blast the soil with so many chemicals that the next generation doesn't want to farm, and guess what? They've boosted GDP.

175

We are obsessed with a metric that doesn't tell the whole truth. It's a terrible relationship to be in, and it's become increasingly abusive of people and the planet.

Thankfully, there are innovators who continue to not only call this out but to act on it around the world.

The Value of the B Corp Certification

There is an entire movement growing to address the injustice of externalized costs, again, not a moment, but a movement. The *B Corp certification* recognizes that business, whether they want to admit it or not, have an impact beyond the bottom line. Some companies take responsibility for that impact, and others don't. The B Corp certification takes full responsibility.

So what exactly is the B Corp certification? It was established by an organization called B Lab. They were recognized as one of Fast Company's Most Innovative Companies in 2020 (B Lab, 2020) and believe an equitable and inclusive work environment and a diverse, empowered, global team are key to achieving economic systems change.

A B Corp, also known as a Certified B Corporation, is a business with verified standards that involve a corporation's social and environmental performance and its impact on customers and employees. It's an extraordinary certification to obtain, and then once you're done, your company is reviewed every three years to ensure you are maintaining the standards, which address equity, inclusion, diversity, environmental stewardship, and so much more.

After a company receives its B Corp certification, it amends its legal governing documents to require its board of directors to balance profit and purpose.

I am proud to call Lorene Arey, the board chair for B Lab North America and Canada, a friend. The organization calls itself "a passionate group of standards experts, business analysts, development officers, product and program managers, people and culture specialists, partnership managers, storytellers, strategists, and engineers."

If you've been through the B Corp certification, which I have and we did at rePlant Capital, you'll know how intense the process is. The scrutiny is fierce and requires full dedication from the team. Our point person from our team managed the day to day of the process and did an extraordinary job. We were fairly quick through the process, accomplishing the certification in about a year. Farms I've worked with have done the same, recognizing that there are others, beyond shareholders, who bear responsibility for an organization's actions.

Is it a perfect standard? Not at all. There is controversy around it too. But the growing success of this movement has had a tremendous impact on the broader business community. It shows that you can build a better, more responsible business, one mindful of all stakeholders, mindful of equity, and continue to operate a profitable and successful business.

In other words, it refutes the naysayers who say that it's not the job of a business to be mindful of its impact on people and the planet.

It's proving otherwise and changing the conversation. It is becoming clear where policy can also play a role, too.

As Michael Ryan, CEO of Dalmore Capital, a London investment company, said to *HR Magazine*, "The purpose of a business used to be to generate profits for its shareholders, almost full stop. And if you dared suggest objectives that were not consistent with dividends and profits, you'd be shouted down. But the world has changed. The general view now is that CEOs are accountable to the public" (Bernard, 2022).

Patagonia recently restructured into a perpetual purpose trust, the Patagonia Trust, which will continue the business, protecting the company's mission and operating model into the future, even after all members of the Chouinard family have stepped away or passed on.

A growing number of businesses, including my friend and serial entrepreneur Seth Goldman, recognize this changing landscape and are answering to the public while solving some of society's gnarliest issues.

Goldman is the cofounder of seven-time Inc. 5000 honoree *Honest Tea*, which sold to Coca-Cola in 2011. His entire career has been focused on bringing better-for-you products to market. Honest Tea created Honest Kids, a juice box with less sugar for kids. When Goldman and his team got those juice boxes into McDonald's Happy Meals, a radical move for an organic beverage brand, and one that had plenty of naysayers, that one partnership removed a billion calories from kids' diets.

I invited him to kick off my MBA course at Rice University a few years ago, during COVID-19, with a virtual keynote, and he crushed it. We opened the invitation to the students at the Leeds School of Business at the University of Colorado, and they loved it too. He is the real deal, honest, authentic, and humble. He cofounded the vegan fast-casual chain PLNT Burger and the nutritious snack company Eat the Change. Eat the Change created a program in 2020 that makes annual donations to nonprofits that promote climate-friendly eating. Everything he does is an extension of his values.

After doing a case study about Coca-Cola versus Pepsi for a competitive strategies class, he discovered plenty of high-sugar, high-calorie drinks and a bunch of water on the market but few beverages in the middle (Hyman, 1998). He thought about creating a low-calorie drink but did not launch the idea for another three years. He was in New York City with a friend, and while eating together, they realized that all of the drinks on the menu were loaded with sugar. So Goldman emailed a former Yale professor, Barry Nalebuff, asking him if the low-calorie beverage idea was still a good one. Nalebuff mentored Goldman and together they created the new tea. Nalebuff provided most of the $500,000 in seed funding, while Goldman contributed a smaller amount after fundraising from his friends and family (Hyman, 1998). Nalebuff came up with the name "Honest Tea," which sounds like "honesty" (Birchall, 2009). And like countless entrepreneurs before him, Goldman built an office in the guest bedroom of his home.

When Coca-Cola decided to discontinue Honest Tea, Goldman flew into action, leveraging both his expertise and network and launched Just Ice Tea, a low-sugar, organic tea line, to replace it. Everything he'd learned the first time around—the successes and mistakes—enabled him to launch a new company and product line in record time. In other words, he took a failure, the discontinuation of his beloved brand, and turned it into a success. A reminder, once again, that the only failure is in failing to learn any lessons.

More recently, Goldman shared some profoundly powerful advice. All of his companies have a mission-driven focus, and in an interview (Ryan, 2023), Goldman was asked for his advice for being idealistic but pragmatic at the same time. He shared, "You have to listen to the market to make sure you're bringing something it wants but doesn't have. It's like water flowing down a hill. You don't know exactly where it's going to go, but the market will lead you where it makes sense . . . and (you have) to find a balance between listening to the market and not listening to the easiest answer."

Like my friend Nicole Poindexter, Goldman is an incredible listener. On incorporating sustainability into a company, Goldman shared: "You have to figure out where your biggest areas of impact are and what you can do about them."

One of the biggest mistakes a company or entrepreneur will make is trying to be all things to all people. Figure out what lights you up, the thing that is going to get you out of bed on the hardest and darkest days, and move toward energizing that. Goldman embodies plant-based living. Everything he's done has pointed toward that North Star. It's a smart approach, as it allows a synergy to play into the work that he does, from establishing production lines to building out a cap table.

In other words, don't try to be all things to all people. If someone well-meaningly suggests, "Be more like (fill in the blank)," you can thank them, study that idea, person, or innovation, then bring your own talents, network, and skills forward. Know your unique value proposition and deliver it. And mitigate your risks and liabilities by not externalizing costs. If you think about it, there really are no longer "externalized" costs because we now know the price we are paying as we destroy the environment and natural resources. And increasingly, the visibility and transparency into these actions presents a brand with either an opportunity or a risk.

Staying Lean

Perhaps Goldman's best advice came for someone who is bootstrapping it and raising money: "Don't set your goals too high too early. If you have to raise $500,000, that's a lot. But if you have to raise $5,000 to get that first test with a store, that's more doable. Then, just keep moving forward and addressing what you can address with the money you have. As long as you keep demonstrating that the concept works, and that it's making financial sense, getting to that next step isn't that hard."

A child doesn't learn to walk all at once, and the same strategy applies here. Take baby steps. Learn to walk before you run. Scaling too quickly, either geographically, with product launches and SKUs, with your team, will risk your model and your financials. Don't let your ego govern your decision-making. Get really quiet and make decisions based on what is best for your long-term viability, not the short-term hit for the ego.

It's obvious on the one hand and yet too many don't follow this advice. If we're going to be talking about sustainability, conservation, and mindfulness, shouldn't that start with the burn rate of a company? Where can you get creative? How can you leverage your existing network, not just for fundraising introductions, but also for feedback, as a focus group?

Too often as entrepreneurs, it's easy to get out over our skis, to get in front of ourselves, to think we need to raise extra money and hire extra team members, anticipating big changes. My advice? And this comes from years of being in the trenches and making this mistake—don't do anything until you are absolutely certain that you are ready for it. Don't hire in anticipation, hire in response. Because as Arlan Hamilton and others have shared, at any moment, an investor may change her mind. I've experienced it, and countless other entrepreneurs and founders have too. You are anticipating an investor coming in, and suddenly, markets change, a family situation changes, something changes, and investors are either pulling out or cutting their investment in half. You will be so glad that you stayed lean and humble.

Other People's Money

Some of the best advice I got was to treat other people's money like it's your own. Be as prudent and mindful of how you spend that cash as you are with your own spending. If you have a burn rate that you yourself would not fund in another company, then do something about it—cut back, slow hiring. For women, this may be more intuitive, since we only get two cents of every dollar invested in venture capital. We have to be so careful with the capital we raise. Perhaps that is why female-led companies outperform, because the lack of access to capital forces them to stay lean. The very best, regardless of gender, race, or ethnicity, are going to value your money like it's their own and proceed mindfully with every dollar spent. Staying lean will invite in a creativity that will serve you well.

So how do you do that? You lean into the conversations on your social media channels for insight. You talk to your customers, your followers, and your investors, because when you are starting, you don't have a budget for focus groups, extensive travel, and consumer research, so you have to leverage your existing relationships and skills.

Build Connections

Partnerships and relationship building is as much of an art as a science. You can build spreadsheets with names and resources, accountability and actions, but importantly, you must remember that you are dealing with humans, with real human needs. Connect with people in that way; ask about their children, their pets, their parents. Remember personal information that they've shared; make notes. Remember the kid in all of us and that we want to feel seen and heard. Kindness and empathy are valuable assets on a team and in a business.

Some of the most game-changing opportunities in my career came from my social media channels. One of the most powerful examples was when I launched the #Epigate campaign. As I've shared, my advocacy began in the food allergy space when my fourth child was diagnosed with food allergies just ahead of her first birthday. With that life-changing event, like millions of others with food allergies, she was prescribed an EpiPen in case of a life-threatening allergic reaction. At that point in time (2006), people weren't quite sure if food allergies were really "a thing" or just moms clamoring for attention. The attitude at the time was very dismissive. And some might say there was a paradigm blindness. So I set about using the data to correct perceptions (similar to what we are now doing here) and to advocate for the millions of families dealing with this condition.

A few years later, I began hearing from thousands of people on my social media platforms about the skyrocketing prices they were suddenly paying for their epinephrine. The prices of the medication had tripled and quadrupled, seemingly overnight, and families couldn't afford them. I was hearing how families had to make trade-offs between car payments and prescriptions, rent and prescriptions, mortgage payments and prescriptions. They could no longer afford both. At the time, I was advocating for clean food for families and investing in organic, and suddenly thought, "If families can't afford lifesaving medication for their kids, brow beating them with facts about why organic is better for them when it's unaffordable is cruel." And it changed everything.

I asked the families contacting me to share their receipts and was flooded with images of what people paid for EpiPens—$600, $700, $800—when the same device cost families in the UK and Canada less than $100. The media picked it up, and suddenly the *New York Times* was covering the story, and I was on Fox News with Liz Claman and her show, *The Claman Countdown*, almost every week, talking about it. In one interview, she asked what needed to happen, and I answered directly: There needs to be a Congressional investigation into the price gouging. And that is exactly what happened. The CEO of Mylan had to testify before Congress.

Liz Claman and her show should have won an Emmy for that. She literally became a warrior for millions of families around the country, advocating for this basic human need, affordable access to a lifesaving medication for a condition that was beyond someone's control. I have no doubt that her work saved countless lives, as she drove awareness of the issue.

Authentic Power

When you are fueled with a purpose and passion larger than your-self, it resonates with an authenticity that you cannot fake. It gives you the power that David R. Hawkins talks about in his book, *Power vs. Force*. And all it takes is some organizational skill, a lot of listen-ing, and unwavering consistency. But when you lock into your pur-pose, it feels like breathing, and your work becomes something you do almost intuitively with clarity and strength, like Liz Claman did.

Which is why I am excited to introduce you to my friend Julia Collins.

Like Seth Goldman of Honest Tea fame, Collins is a serial entrepreneur. She discovered food was her calling as a young girl in San Francisco. She spent her early career building food companies in New York City, brands like Murray's Cheese, Mexicue, Union Square Hospitality Group, and Harlem Jazz Enterprises. She cofounded Zume Pizza and became the first Black woman to create a company valued at more than a billion dollars. Collins holds a BA from Harvard and an MBA from Stanford, and in 2018, she had her first child and locked in on her life's purpose: bringing delicious food to people in a way that helps heal the planet for everyone, including her children.

Collins is now the founder and CEO of Planet FWD, the lead-ing climate management platform for consumer companies, and she's a dear friend. Planet FWD reduces the cost and complexity of creating sustainable products through its proprietary data and soft-ware. The platform provides consumer companies with the tools to understand and reduce their carbon footprint.

The platform is inspired by Planet FWD's own snack brand, Moonshot, which launched in 2020 as the first climate-friendly snack brand. Moonshot was acquired by Patagonia Provisions in 2023, a first for Patagonia in more than 20 years.

In addition to leading Planet FWD, Collins sits on the Climate Collaborative board, the Food for Climate League board, and the advisory council for Launch with GS. She is also an active angel investor focused on funding female entrepreneurs and BIPOC founders. Collins is also an Ambassador for the Smithsonian National Museum of African American History and Culture.

In other words, she is a force for equity and justice.

When you sit down with her, she is full of intellect, empathy, passion, and generations of wisdom. She will speak to her grandmother's influence on her, her parents' influence. She holds people close, and she is unapologetically herself.

According to *Beautiful Economics*, "In traditional economic theory, goods that are scarce are called economic goods. Other goods are called 'free goods' because it is presumed they are in endless abundance. However, the so called 'free goods' like air and water are no longer abundant and no longer free. In fact, the reverse is now true and the 'new scarce' commodities are clean water, unpolluted air, and fertile, unspoiled land" (Collinge, 2021).

Collins knows this. She created Moonshot with the express purpose of building a food brand that was as good for the earth as it was for us. She shared, "We designed Moonshot with the planet in mind at every step of the way, thinking through our impacts with each decision we made, from our ingredients to our supply chain to our packaging and everything in between."

Moonshot Snacks creates crackers from regeneratively grown ingredients. The brand also represents Planet FWD's work in connecting farmers with brands that want to change the world through food. Collins founded Planet FWD and Moonshot to create a better world for her children.

She's not alone, and not only are these models good for her children, they are good for the planet and the company's bottom line.

According to a report by McKinsey & Company (2023), "Over the past five years, products making ESG-related claims accounted for 56% of all growth—about 18% more than would have been expected given their standing at the beginning of the five-year period: products making these claims averaged 28% cumulative growth over the five-year period, versus 20% for products that made no such claims. As for the CAGR (compound annual growth rate), products with ESG-related claims boasted a 1.7 percentage-point advantage—a significant amount in the context of a mature and modestly growing industry—over products without them. Products making ESG-related claims therefore now account for nearly half of all retail sales in the categories examined."

Following on the early discussion about "ESG" and the values represented, the McKinsey report goes on to state, "It is of course paramount for the development of a sustainable and inclusive economy that companies back any ESG-related claims they make with genuine actions. *Greenwashing*—empty or misleading claims about the environmental or social merits of a product or service—poses reputational risks to businesses by eroding the trust of consumers. It also compromises their ability to make more environmentally and socially responsible choices, and potentially undermines the role of regulators."

In other words, yes, anyone can make bogus ESG claims, but it's presenting a liability, which is clearly not your fiduciary duty. And there are plenty of companies out there right now who are doing exactly this, greenwashing, carbon washing, even gender and justice washing—pretending to be something that they are not, failing to invest in the underlying infrastructure to support meaningful integration and change.

"The research shows that a wide range of consumers across incomes, life stages, ages, races, and geographies are buying products bearing ESG-related labels—with an average of plus or minus

15% deviation across demographic groups for environmentally and socially conscious buyers compared with the total population. This suggests that the appeal of environmentally and socially responsible products isn't limited to niche audiences and is making genuine headway with broad swaths of America" (McKinsey & Company, 2023). In other words, we are all paying attention.

According to Bloomberg's ESG Data Acquisition and Management Survey 2023, more than 90% of executives are increasing investments in ESG data. Why? Consumers want sustainability and investors want to reduce portfolio risks. "Once categorized as an alternative data source, ESG data has quickly become integral to the value financial firms deliver to their clients." These values matter to your bottom line.

Google sees it too, with the way that we are accessing information. Kate Brandt, Google's chief sustainability officer, often highlights how we are using Google's Timelapse to understand our changing climate and environment. She shared in an interview, "We think about Timelapse as having a similar power to educate, inspire, and show people visually what's been happening on our planet" (Farra, 2021). The product is designed to show us exactly what climate change looks like.

According to David A. Cifrino (2023), "New regulations expected to be adopted in 2023 will result in exponential growth in the amount of environmental, social, and governance (ESG), i.e., sustainability, data generated by reporting companies and available to investors. The U.S. Securities and Exchange Commission (SEC) is expected to adopt final rules requiring detailed disclosure by companies of climate-related risks and opportunities by the end of 2023. The newly-formed International Sustainability Standards Board (ISSB) is expected to adopt two reporting standards: one on climate-related risks, and a second on other sustainability related information. Regardless of how much harmonization there will be between these and other ESG disclosure standards, it is clear that mandatory, standardized sustainability reporting by corporations will increase significantly worldwide over the next few years."

In other words, the data is coming, and we may package it and label it in different ways, but this demand for transparency is going to drive change.

Accountability Is Coming

The demand for enhanced ESG disclosure is intense. Don't get tied up with the letters. Pay attention to the values. When you see "ESG," think "risk mitigation." Are you investing in people, practices and policies that amplify opportunities or liabilities? Are you investing in people, practices and policies that are building a livable future? Globally, overall ESG investing is massive, having grown as much as tenfold in the last decade. Morningstar, Inc. estimated that total assets in ESG-designated funds totaled more than US$3.9 trillion at the end of September 2021. The evolution in ESG investing has been accompanied by exponential growth in the amount and types of data available for ESG investors to consider. The number of public companies publishing corporate sustainability reports grew from less than 20 in the early 1990s to more than 10,000 companies today, and about 90% of the Fortune Global 500 have set carbon emission targets, up from 30% in 2009.

According to Impakt IQ, a company that addresses ESG blind spots and provides insight into business impacts, in order to leverage this intelligence to make informed decisions, "Demand for sustainability and ESG information is steadily increasing and becoming a regulatory requirement. Therefore, business leaders need a way to evaluate, measure, manage, and communicate to stakeholders ESG strategies, risks, and performance relative to material ESG issues. ESG scores are that measure." According to the Impakt IQ team, "The current problem is ESG scores are largely derived by outside analysts and artificial intelligence algorithms searching the Internet for company-related ESG practices and reports associated with that company. These scores are subjective at best and leave companies vulnerable and at high risk due to misinformation, inconsistent, not auditable, and inaccurate ESG scores." The company has developed a reporting system that can be viewed beside your financial statement, providing insight into critical financial and reputational risks of an organization, along with value creation opportunities.

The foundation of the methodology is based on the most relevant ESG frameworks in the world: Task Force for Climate Change Disclosure (TCFD), Sustainability Accounting Standards Board (SASB), International Sustainability Standards Board (ISSB), and the SEC. The company is founded by Elisa Taylor, who has been recognized as "A Top 50 Leader" by the World Summit on Innovation and Entrepreneurship, listed by Gartner as a top five "Cool Vendors" in sustainable business solutions, and was a member of the UN Global Compact Business Leaders' Summit on Sustainable Business Solutions.

The National Academies of Sciences, Engineering, and Medicine (2023) just released a new report outlining a comprehensive plan for the United States to achieve net-zero carbon emissions by 2050 while ensuring equity and justice in the energy transition. It covers a wide range of areas, including clean energy, public health, workforce development, and more.

The Academies' key recommendations are as follows:

- Broaden climate policies beyond subsidies
- Prioritize equity and health in energy decisions
- Strengthen the U.S. electricity grid
- Establish rigorous data analysis for transparency

- Engage local communities in infrastructure planning
- Reform financial markets for climate projects
- Build a skilled workforce
- Update targets for industry and buildings
- Invest in research and development
- Manage the future of the fossil fuel sector

Their fourth call to action is to establish rigorous data analysis for transparency. Why does this type of integrity in the data matter? Because there are plenty of people currently trying to game it.

Scope 0 and Avoiding Bogus Claims

There is an increasing demand for transparency around greenhouse gas (GHG) emissions. As you probably know, these disclosures are called Scope 1, 2, and 3. There is also a growing call to disclose lobbying dollars as it relates to GHG emissions. Some are calling this disclosure "Scope 0." It makes sense. It's the earliest indication of a company's commitment to its environmental initiatives. Is it lobbying for or against climate solutions? Consumers want to know, and so do workers and employees. It gets back to that data for the planet. Scope 0 is a leading indicator of a company's climate goals and intentions.

Why does this matter? According to McKinsey (2023),

Products that made the least prevalent claims (such as "vegan" or "carbon zero") grew 8.5% more than peers that didn't make them. Products making medium-prevalence claims (such as "sustainable packaging" or "plant-based") had a 4.7% growth differential over their peers. The most prevalent claims (such as "environmentally sustainable") corresponded with the smallest growth differential. Yet even products making these widespread claims still enjoyed roughly 2% higher growth than products that didn't make them, suggesting that commonplace claims can be differentiating.

On top of capturing market share, products that carry these claims also engender customer loyalty and support recurring revenue and repeat purchases, according to an analysis of NielsenIQ's household panel data: "Brands that garner more than half of their sales from products making ESG-related claims enjoy 32 to 34 percent repeat rates (meaning that buyers purchase products from the brand three or more times annually)." By contrast, brands that receive less than 50 percent of their sales from products that make ESG-related claims achieve repeat rates of under 30 percent. This difference does not prove that consumers reward brands because of ESG-related claims, but it does suggest that a deeper engagement with ESG-related issues across a brand's portfolio might enhance consumer loyalty toward the brand as a whole. Products making multiple types of claims grew about twice as fast as products that made only one.

But again, you can't bullshit your consumer. We live in an age of Instagram and TikTok, where videos and information go viral and the power lies in the social media hands of millions. It reminds me of when General Mills acquired Annie's. I was working with the Annie's team at the time, and what happened can only be described as the Internet puking all over the brands. The acquisition was announced, and within a few hours, tens of thousands of comments were posted to Annie's social media pages, with blistering criticism on the company "selling out." I'd known this company for years; I know Annie herself, the mom who founded it. And the amount of comments unleashed on the company resembled a tsunami of hate. Rather than cut and paste a standardized answer, which is often a corporate response to a PR crisis, Annie's team engaged as humans. They buckled up, hunkered down, and responded to every comment. It saved the brand.

Your actions will speak far louder than your words (or any label or press release), and the European Union is already drafting legislation to make these greenwashing claims illegal. If you make a promise to your consumer, follow through.

Diversifying Your Cap Table

Like Denise Woodard at Partake Foods, Collins's focus at Planet FWD extends beyond conservation and protecting people and the planet. It incorporates diversity at its core. She shares, "Founders have the power to address structural racism in the tech world. It's not just who you hire and promote. It's who makes it to your cap table. When I founded Planet FWD, I was determined to diversify mine. At my first round, 9% of my investors were women and people of color. I'm in the business of making great products and in the business of creating climate impact. But I'm also in the business of creating returns for my investors. Intergenerational wealth transfer and wealth creation are two of the most important levers for expanding equality. I am committed to creating opportunities for underrepresented investors. There needs to be more room in the tech world for all of us. Our starting points are (1) diversify who we invest in; (2) diversify our investors."

Diversity is good for your bottom line, and it starts with your investors.

But let's pause for a minute and a quick overview of the fundraising process. I don't want you to feel uninformed or let anyone make you feel stupid when you step into this. The venture capital world will sometimes behave as if they are the smartest guys in the room. It can be a condescending approach. The more you know, the more powerfully you can negotiate, so here is a quick overview on fundraising. I'll add this in an appendix, as an easy reference too.

More often than not, you see entrepreneurs bootstrapping, where you use the revenue generated by the business or your own funds. One of the most successful examples of this is Sara Blakely of Spanx. She didn't take outside money. She started her company with hustle and a few thousand dollars.

You can also turn to friends and family who believe in what you are doing. They know you and can get behind your vision, but you will probably have to answer to them at every family gathering, so be mindful of who you reach out to here.

The next outreach might be to angel investors who usually request an equity stake in the company in exchange for their capital. Again, be mindful of who you want to enter into a relationship with. Putting someone on your cap table is a serious commitment.

You can also turn to crowdfunding platforms like Indiegogo and Kickstarter.

And then, there are the venture capital firms who invest in high growth startups. Here are the different "rounds," the funding rounds that may be required, as you grow your company.

Funding Series	Typical Capital Raised	Company Stage
Series A	$2 million to $15 million	Early stage
Series B	$10 million to $60 million	Expansion stage
Series C	$20 million to $100 million	Growth stage
Series D	$30 million to $150 million	Late-stage

Other options for funding are Small Business Administration (SBA) Loans, which are government-backed loans that support small businesses. These loans tend to have lower interest rates and better terms than other loans. And you can also look into grants that can provide funding for specific needs.

Again, this is really straightforward. It's not complicated so don't let anyone make you feel small. Familiarizing yourself with the language around this will help.

So what's another industry ripe for this type of innovation and disruption? The fashion and apparel industry, which is why I am going to introduce you to my friend Lewis Perkins.

If I was early in this work to clean up our food system, Perkins was early on the need to clean up apparel and fashion. We've been riding parallel tracks on this journey for the last 25 years, and he is now the president of the Apparel Impact Institute (Aii).

I learned about the connection between food and fashion when I was studying genetically engineered crops. Cotton is one of the largest genetically engineered crops. It is often planted in the same fields where peanuts grow. It's called crop rotation, when peanuts are planted in a field during one season, and then cotton is planted in the same field during another. Whatever is done to one crop impacts the soil and land that both crops are growing in. So whatever is being done to cotton is going to impact the soil that peanuts are growing in.

Aii identifies, funds, scales, and measures the apparel and footwear industry's proven environmental impact solutions. It plays the critical role of a technical clearinghouse for partner brands, manufacturers, and philanthropic donors, validating and aggregating proven environment initiatives. Their focus areas are energy, water, and chemistry.

According to Aii's report, "The global fashion industry is a multi-trillion dollar industry, producing over 100 billion garments annually. Given its size and nature, the industry faces a number of social and environmental challenges. The key environmental challenges are complex and interrelated, but most broadly fall under land use, water use, chemical use, biodiversity loss, and greenhouse gas (GHG) emissions. Recent publications have estimated the GHG emissions associated with the fashion industry—with figures ranging from between 2–8% of annual global emissions" (Ley, van Mazijk, Hugill, Perkins, and Gaines, 2021).

The report goes on to state that in order to mobilize billions in capital and "to overcome barriers, a concerted effort is needed by five key stakeholder groups: financiers (debt and equity), manufacturers, brands, philanthropy, and governments." The report echoes the World Bank, European Central Bank, asset managers, and others calling for change.

Defining Your Scope

As a refresher, according to the division of Greenhouse Gas Emissions and GHG Protocol (2015), emissions are given the following definitions:

- **Scope 1:** Direct emissions (emissions from owned and controlled facilities)
- **Scope 2:** Indirect emissions (emissions from the generation of purchased energy, steam, heat, and/or cooling)
- **Scope 3:** Emissions that occur in the value chain of the company (not included in Scope 2 emissions), including upstream and downstream emissions

Examples of upstream emissions include emissions of purchased goods and services, transport of supplies, and business travel. Examples of downstream emissions include transportation of products, use of sold products, and product disposal (think of the piles of clothing waste that you can see in landfills).

As Ley et al. shared, "Given Scopes 1 and 2—direct and indirect emissions—are under direct control of an organization, they are easier to measure and report. However, the complex and fragmented nature of fashion supply chains means that Scope 3—indirect value chain emissions, which represent the vast majority of emissions—have, up until recently, been somewhat overlooked and are typically the least reported."

Emissions in Scopes 1 and 2 only account for approximately 3%–5% of an organization's total GHG emissions. In many industries,

Scope 3 often represents an organization's most significant greenhouse gas impact. The fashion industry is no different; on average, 96% of emissions stem from Scope 3 across those fashion brands with approved science-based targets (SBTs). Within Scope 3 emissions, more than 78% come from upstream emissions—purchased goods and services—with the remaining 22% from downstream emissions.

There is also an increasing call to action for companies to disclose their lobbying efforts and expenditures. "There are many examples of companies lobbying against the very kinds of green initiatives they are undertaking" (Vanham, 2023). And given what we've seen from fashion to food, it makes sense.

Aii's goal is to help their partners in the fashion and apparel industries address this. So the way I've spent my entire career focused on tackling some of the food industry's greatest challenges, my dear friend Lewis Perkins has done the same in apparel and fashion.

Not surprisingly, there is an overlap, and we've both worked with Target Corporation. I was invited in years ago, when they began reformulating their private label food products, and they were the organization that reached out to Perkins in an effort to get a handle on what was happening with its supply chains, and where it could do better. In collaboration with Aii, Target and other partners came together to address the emissions coming out of their supply chains, to measure them, and to build accountability. When I spoke with Perkins about it, and his role as a leader, I asked him what he'd learned. He was really honest and shared how he figured it out by building out a well-rounded team, learning how to check in and not micro-manage, learning how to lead and not project. I asked him what he considered to be the single most important practice he engages in, to keep his head on straight with all of the pressure. He paused and said, "My sobriety. I stopped drinking 30 years ago."

It reminded me of the Athletic Brewing guys and the growth of NoLo beverages. Perkins clearly isn't alone. With all of the biohacking going on and focus of business leaders on longevity, sobriety can be a superpower.

Where Do You Start?

It was Seneca who said, "We learn not in school but in life."

So what can you and your company do? Build boards that mitigate against environmental risks and social risks by engaging leaders with diverse experiences. Leverage tools so that decision-making is data-driven and measured. Build a board that reflects gender, equity, social, and environmental values—the values that are defining and changing the landscape of business.

Why? Because the governance of your company, and the principles under which it operates, determine so much. Lean into a diversity of solutions and smarter technology. More than 14 million tons of clothing is either landfilled or incinerated every year, according to the EPA. It represents almost 6% of all solid waste in the United States. The opportunity to drive change in every industry is enormous, including apparel. Refiberd recently raised a $3.4 million seed round to use its AI to tackle textile waste and sorting textiles in order to enable true textile-to-textile recycling. There are so many opportunities to engage here.

Ignoring the problem also ignores the solution.

According to a report by the Latino Donor Collaborative in partnership with Wells Fargo, "Latino consumers' economic power in the United States was resilient through COVID-19 and keeps growing, reaching $3.2 trillion in 2021" (Gomez, 2023). For context, that means Latino GDP in the United States has now overtaken the economic output of the United Kingdom and India (Contreras, 2021). It's expected to challenge Germany's and Japan's next.

The Latino Donor Collaborative report also found that, from 2011 to 2021, annualized wage growth and spending grew twice as quickly among people who identify as Hispanic or Latino compared to those who do not. During that decade, the U.S. Latino population became the world's third-fastest-growing economy, trailing only China and India.

If you don't have a diversity of voices on your team, on your cap table, and in your boardroom, you are going to miss so much.

I remember giving a keynote to a large multinational that had just been acquired by a foreign company. The CEO of the foreign company gave his keynote that morning, and I followed later that afternoon.

When I was done, he approached me and said, "I had no idea that 1% of the farmland in the United States is organic," a point I often make in keynotes, since 85% of consumers are purchasing something organic at least some of the time. He'd just purchased an organic company, paying hundreds of millions of dollars for it. How had he missed this? Later that evening, I pulled up his board of directors. They all looked exactly the same, dressed exactly the same. One gender, one race, almost in uniform.

Paradigm blindness. There it was again. You don't know what you don't know. We are way stronger as a fabric woven together than we are as any single thread.

Get comfortable being uncomfortable. Explore what's missing and learn how to weave things together. It's where both learning and growth happen.

Remember how nature taught us that homogeneous systems fail? Any time a company has a horrific mess in the media, I pull up the link to their board of directors, to understand who is governing and how this might have impacted and influenced leadership's behavior and actions. If you don't have that diversity on your board, you're at risk for blind spots. Not only will you miss risks but also opportunities. And more often than not, you can tell a lot about a company's culture and values by the diversity of its board, gender, age, experience, and industry. The more diverse a board of directors is, the deeper the experience it brings to problem-solving.

Follow Your Values

A company without clear values is a company without a compass. And there have been countless examples of failures here, with companies checking the ESG and DEI boxes, without meaningful commitment to the underlying values. It opens them to backlash, they aren't grounded in the principles to defend themselves against the accusations, and too often, end up backpedaling, losing customers on all sides of the issue.

As Alison Taylor often shares on LinkedIn and in podcasts, "If you turn on a dime based on social media reactions, you will look skittish and lacking direction. Not only that, but it encourages political grandstanding and suggests CEOs have no solid anchor and will overreact to whoever is yelling at them today . . . . Rather than resorting to governance based on public opinion, a much better idea is to have clear values and data-driven metrics that you can use to support your company's positions."

Stephanie Harlow (2023) shares how social platforms are also now used as search engines, increasing their stickiness and relevance in our lives. One generation will use Google as a search engine; another generation will use TikTok.

There is so much noise, which is why Jessica Yellin launched "News Not Noise." A key part of any business leader's job is building a trusted list of resources, places, and people that you turn to for unbiased information, so that you can make the most informed choice when it comes to your products.

If those people all look the same, chances are high that you are going to have several blind spots and expose your business to unnecessary risk. Rather than view this diversity, equity, and inclusion or ESG metrics as a quota to hit, a box-checking exercise, or a trend, recognize that it is your fiduciary duty.

I hope you're starting to catch some themes here. In the wise words of Maya Angelou, "Do the best you can until you know better. Then when you know better, do better."

You now know better.

Action Steps: Values Inventory

What values do you hold dear? What is your most important value, your North Star? Your North Star is going to serve as your compass, throughout your life. When I was a kid, heading off to college, my dad took me aside and said, "Never compromise who you are." I can still hear him saying it. It's been a guiding principle my entire career.

The three most important values to me are integrity, truth, and loyalty, but if I am ever in a position where I am asked to compromise my integrity for loyalty, I will break the bond. I don't care if I've been in a relationship for five months, five years, or 25 years. If I am asked to compromise my integrity, I am out. It's my North Star. So I want you to make a list of your values, figure out which one is your North Star, and align yourself with people who share that value. How much do you value integrity? How much do you value truth? Are there other things that are more important to you? Find those who share your values. These values will serve as a compass as you move forward.

Resources

B Lab. (n.d.). *B Lab is a fast company world's most innovative company for 2020 in the not-for-profit category* [press release]. Available at: https://www.bcorporation.net/en-us/news/press/worlds-most-innovative-company-fast-company-2020/

Bernard, D. (2022). Rise in CEOs linking pay to engagement and diversity targets. *HR Magazine* [online]. Available at: https://www.hrmagazine.co.uk/content/news/rise-in-ceos-linking-pay-to-engagement-and-diversity-targets/

Bishay, K. (2017). The importance of accountability. *HR Magazine* [online]. Available at: https://www.hrmagazine.co.uk/content/features/the-importance-of-accountability

Bloomberg and Adox Research. (2023). *ESG data acquisition & management survey 2023*. Available at: https://assets.bbhub.io/professional/sites/10/Bloomberg-ESG-Data-Acquisition-and-Management-Survey-2023.pdf

Cifrino, D. (2023). *The rise of international ESG disclosure standards* [online]. Harvard Law School Forum on Corporate Governance. Available at: https://corpgov.law.harvard.edu/2023/06/29/the-rise-of-international-esg-disclosure-standards/

Collinge, H. (2021). *Beautiful economics: A guide to gentle world domination.* Simon & Schuster.

Contreras, R. (2021). *U.S. Latino economic output closing in on Germany* [graph]. Axios. Available at: https://www.axios.com/2023/09/27/us-latino-economic

Farra, E. (2021). Google's head of sustainability wants you to see the earth in a new way. *Vogue* [online]. Available at: https://www.vogue.com/article/google-earth-timelapse-climate-change-tool-kate-brandt

Gomez, B. (2023). *U.S. Latino economic output grows to $3.2 trillion, according to new study* [online]. CNBC. Available at: https://www.cnbc.com/2023/09/27/us-latino-economic-output-grows-to-3point2-trillion-new-study-says.html

Harlow, S. (2023). *How effective are ads on social media?* [online]. GWI. Available at: https://blog.gwi.com/trends/ads-on-social-media/

Hyman, J. (1998, Sept. 14). Honest tea company fills niche with natural low-cal alternative. *Washington Times*. Available at: https://archive.ph /20190607090703/https://www.questia.com/read/1G1-56776275 /honest-tea-company-fills-niche-with-natural-low-cal

Ley, K., van Mazijk, R., Hugill, R., Perkins, L., and Gaines, R. (2021). *Unlocking the trillion-dollar fashion decarbonisation opportunity: Existing and innovative solutions.* Apparel Impact Institute. Available at: https://apparelimpact.org/wp-content/uploads/2021/11/Aii _UnlockingTheTrillion-DollarFashionDecarbonisationOpportunity _Report_v11.pdf

McKinsey & Company. (2023). *Consumers care about sustainability—and back it up with their wallets* [online.] Available at: https://www.mckinsey .com/industries/consumer-packaged-goods/our-insights/consumers -care-about-sustainability-and-back-it-up-with-their-wallets

National Academies of Sciences, Engineering, and Medicine. (2023). *New report provides comprehensive plan to meet U.S. net-zero goals and ensure fair and equitable energy transition* [online]. Available at: https:// www.nationalacademies.org/news/2023/10/new-report-provides -comprehensive-plan-to-meet-u-s-net-zero-goals-and-ensure-fair -and-equitable-energy-transition

Ryan, K. J. (2023). Honest Tea's Seth Goldman shares the secrets of scaling with the founder of a mission-driven pet brand. *Inc.* [online]. Available at: https://www.inc.com/magazine/202309/kevin-j-ryan /woofbowl-built-a-food-truck-for-dogs-honest-teas-seth-goldman -has-experience-driving-growth.html

Vanham, P. (2023, Oct. 5). Why lobbying should be included in ESG ratings. *Fortune*.

www.ft.com. (2009). *Tea and synergy.* [online] Available at: https://www .ft.com/content/ff91273a-550f-11de-b5d4-00144feabdc0

10

Fourteen Steps to Your Personal Sustainability Plan

"If you can build a muscle, you can build a mindset."

—Jay Shetty

JUST AS COMPANIES have failed to put clean air and clean water on their balance sheets as assets critical to the success of their businesses, they've also failed to put the health of their founders and CEOs down as assets.

And perhaps, even more importantly, while investing in the long-term viability of assets on their balance sheets, many CEOs fail to make the same investments in themselves.

My friend Jen Fisher is the human sustainability leader at Deloitte. It's a role that she created for the company after both experiencing and witnessing record burnout. Companies focus on the conditions of their assets all the time. Absenteeism and productivity directly impact the bottom line, and employees, executives and CEOs are some of the most valuable assets.

You Are on the Balance Sheet

As a founder, you are an incredibly valuable asset in your model and on your balance sheet, and you have to remember to value yourself that way. Why? Because your mental, emotional, physical, and spiritual health all impact how you show up for work. You are going to present as either an asset or a liability, so let's make sure you show up in the asset column! It reminds me of when I met Martha Stewart very early in my career. She was taking her company public. She was *the* asset of the company, and when my team at Invesco met with her, someone asked, "What happens if something happens to you?" None of us could have seen what was coming, but the question remains as one of the most important that was asked in that meeting.

Her answer? "My mother is still very much active and alive. I don't plan on going anywhere anytime soon."

I don't think anyone could have anticipated what would happen next. We rarely can.

When one of my best friends was diagnosed with stage IV lung cancer at the height of his success in private equity, I could not have anticipated getting that phone call from him, and then five years later, sitting at the side of his bed in the hospital with him, a few days before he died. It seemed unfathomable. He had "everything"—a beautiful family, an amazing wife and sons, and he was a titan in the real estate and investment worlds. When I walked into that hospital room, a few weeks before he died, he said, "Oh my gosh, oh my gosh, oh my gosh." And I sat with him and his wife, knowing it was the last time I would see him. His death woke me up to how precious every minute of this life is and how none of us really know how long we have.

We get to choose who we surround ourselves with. Choose the ones who have your back, who share your name in rooms you are not in, and who want to see you succeed and celebrate your success when you do. And then, support them too.

Which is exactly what I did for my friend with cancer. I had his back, the way he had always had mine. When he was first diagnosed, he wanted help cleaning up his diet, but I told him that he'd also have to get the junk out of his head. He got very quiet and said, "That's going to be a lot harder to do." And I told him that *that* is the work.

Which brings me to what is probably the most important section in this book. Investing in your mental, physical, emotional, and spiritual health like your company depends on it. Because it does. It's your fiduciary duty. And I don't think enough founders, teams, and investors understand just how important this is. But it's a question I ask every founder, "What do you do to take care of yourself? Especially when things get hard?"

We live in a hustle and grind culture, like Mike Cessario at Liquid Death shared earlier. Nothing is going to burn through your creativity faster than relentlessly driving yourself into the ground. Creativity is contingent on imagination. And imagination needs room to breathe. If you're working from 5 a.m. until 1 a.m. every day, broadcasting the grind, you're grinding down one of your company's most important assets—your health.

And if you go down, if you get sick, you can't run a company, much less be successful. And whether we realize it or not, how we treat ourselves says everything about how we treat other people in our lives.

So this is going to get a bit personal. You may like what it says and you may want to throw the book at the wall. Again, as I've echoed over and over in this book—your authenticity matters. These suggestions are coming from a very deep lived experience, mine, others who have navigated this, mentors and role models, and those who have been close to me on this journey. They're not prescriptions, but suggestions. Take these as guidelines. Maybe you want to embrace all of them now, maybe some of them, maybe none of them. Consider it a resource that you can turn back toward at a later date, should you need it.

But promise me that you will remind yourself of this often, that you will put this on a sticky note on your mirror: "My health is an asset. Invest accordingly."

You have a fiduciary duty to your investors to take care of your health. It's part of your job.

Best Practices to Prevent a Toxic Leak

Rarely does the world give permission for founders to invest in their health, but it's one of the most important investments you can make. You are on the balance sheet. Failure to address your health from the inside out can create an acute crisis like a heart attack, and it can also create what I think of as a "toxic leak." You've probably seen or experienced it at some point in your life. This toxic leak can show up in someone as depression, anxiety, addiction, aggression, anger, and other destructive behaviors that not only impact your health but also the relationships around you. This leak can be corrosive to a team, a culture, and so much more. Your job as a founder, innovator, and entrepreneur is to take care of your company's assets. You are one of the assets, and so are your employees.

The next sections cover a few suggestions.

Sleep

When I started my first organization, AllergyKids Foundation, I had four kids under the age of six, none stood higher than my waistline, and in the juggling act of motherhood and work, I sacrificed sleep.

We all know its value; I don't need to preach that to you. So what I will say is when you do sleep, make sure it is the best sleep you can possibly get. Use earplugs, an eye mask, shut out light, noise, and set the temperature to the level where you can relax the most. Don't go to bed on a full stomach. Log off, if you can (I know, the addiction is real) a few hours before bedtime. And move your phone away from your head and bed. Then make sure that when you sleep, no matter the number of hours, that it's as true and deep as you can get. We focus so much on the quality of our food, and the quality of our sleep is just as important.

I've learned to use the "3, 2, 1 method." Three hours before bedtime, stop eating. Two hours before bedtime, put away technology, and one hour before bedtime, start to wind down.

We all have chapters in our lives when sleep eludes us, whether it's the birth of our kids, the death of a loved one, or the stress of an unexpected chapter. Life happens and sleep won't always be accessible. Know that each stage of your life is a chapter—some will be long, and some will be short. Some chapters will be brutal and full of pain, and some chapters will be ridiculously beautiful. Put these practices in place, so that whether you are sleeping four hours or eight, you are getting the highest quality sleep you possibly can.

Want to learn more? Check out Andrew Huberman's podcast.

Encouragement

We need to understand the power of support and positive thinking. I'm not talking about toxic positivity. Those days are over. I am talking about the authentically supportive people you have in your life who have your back, the ones who will help you through some of the hardest chapters.

Some have a hype squad in their moms, like Arlan Hamilton. Others have a social media army that they command, like Erin

Gallagher. Still others, like Nicole Poindexter, lean into faith and God as a source of strength and power for her work (always power, given the positive energy and attributes it conveys, over brute force). And friends like Sara Blakely will often share how she turns to Wayne Dyer when she needed a boost of confidence. She recently answered a question on her Instagram feed (which is both a source of brilliant strategy and hilarious family fun) about confidence and self-doubt. She got really candid, which by the comments, was appreciated. She said something along the lines of, "People think because you've accomplished these big things that you don't have self-doubt. I had self-doubt the entire time." The truth is so powerful.

Most people who achieve great things, like "beyond your wildest dreams" great things, learn how to manage that self-doubt. Blakely shared how when these moments would hit her, she'd get in her car and turn on the audio for Wayne Dyer's "No Limit Person" and listen to his advice in those dark times and moments when she was down. And she kept doing it over and over again, reinforcing that positivity and mindset. Her story has been told countless times. But I think that one of the most amazing parts of it is how she shares that her dad encouraged failure. He deliberately asked her and her brother when they got home from school what they failed at that day, because he knew they were trying something new. In other words, he turned failure into something positive. He completely reframed it for the courage required to try something new and the education and lessons gained in the process.

So whether you've got a dad like Blakely, a mom like Arlan, or someone in your life who is a constant source of reflection and light, that positivity and encouragement will be one of your most valuable resources. And if you don't already, show gratitude to those who give it to you.

Because entrepreneurship is an isolating journey at times, and we need a source of encouragement and positivity, especially when things get hard and the naysayers get really loud.

And they will get loud. You are breaking out of the status quo and the box that someone has you in, which is going to make some people uncomfortable. When you level up, you will inevitably create distance with those who knew you before. Remember, you playing small does not serve the world. Neither do small minds and small thinking. They are shackling. Invite in relationships that can grow with you, ones that want to see you expand into your highest potential.

Want to learn more? Follow Wayne Dyer's work. Read *How to Be a No-Limit Person*. And read one of my favorite books, *The Alchemist*, by Paulo Coelho, if you haven't already.

Network

Which brings me to your network. As Arlan shares, relationships, your network, is a currency. And I don't care if you're a 12-year-old starting a lemonade stand, an 18-year-old starting college, a 28-year-old starting your first business, or a 64-year-old writing your first book—building that network starts now.

When I was starting AllergyKids, my consulting firm and rePlant Capital, I had no budget for marketing and public relations and would draft emails to journalists, full of data and statistics, hoping they'd pick up the story. I tried to make it as easy as possible for them to generate an article, layering in data, sourcing the materials, and providing the content. And it worked. I also knew that food allergies were impacting more people than the media was reporting on, as evidenced by the sales of epinephrine, and that the existing data were dated.

But I didn't just spam them. I researched each journalist. I studied the articles they'd written, what they'd covered, and what they cared about. I looked up their bios at the end of their articles, collected email addresses, or searched their columns.

And I personalized the hell out of those emails to them.

And as I found success in the written media, I broadened my approach, reaching out to those at some of the major morning shows. The one that I remember the most vividly was an email I drafted to Jim Bell. He was the executive producer of the *Today Show* at the time. I'd just launched AllergyKids, and somewhere I'd read that he had boys of his own. So in true "Type A" fashion, I drafted an email to him, sharing the data and my vision for kids with food allergies and how to create universal awareness to keep our kids safe.

He replied to that email. It blew me away. He wrote something along the lines of "Thanks so much for your work, Robyn. We are not interested in doing a story on this at this time."

I could not believe that the head of the *Today Show* replied. I had absolute zero public relations or media expertise. And somehow it had broken through. I cannot emphasize enough how much inspiration that gave me to push on, at a time where there were plenty of rejections and naysayers. When my first book, *The Unhealthy Truth*, was published three years later, we debuted it on the *Today Show*.

That formula has continued to serve me, whether I am reaching out to potential investors, new partners in the food industry, or scientists and journalists that I want to connect with.

Build relationships. Personalize your outreach. And once you've connected, make note of pets, children, and names, so that you can personalize the outreach again.

Networks are a powerful resource. It's why I co-founded Women Transforming Food and Finance with my friend, Sarah Day Lavesque of Regenerative Food Systems Investment Forum, and why we are seeing growing attendance at events around the world, from

South Summit, started by my friends at IE University in Spain, to evokeAG, started by friends in Australia. Silos are dangerous in business, and attending new events and networking can help address them.

And when you do, don't pretend to be anyone other than yourself. Your authenticity matters, it's your truth, and it will resonate above all of the noise. If you hide your true self, or mask it, people won't know who they are dealing with, and they won't know how to engage. More importantly, the people who are meant for you won't be able to find you.

And again, every chance you get, show gratitude—for someone taking the time to read your email, to respond, and for those in your network. Gratitude is a powerful asset, so recognize those who support you—listen to and thank them.

Community

This is different to network though similar in that it provides supportive scaffolding to you in this work. While network consists of those in your professional world, community consists of those in your personal life, from places like a book club, church or synagogue, a favorite yoga class, or your friends that you meet to walk, run, or bike with. They tend to be outside of work and yet are foundational to holding you up when things get tough and you need to catch your breath.

Some of the people who've had my back during the hardest times are the dearest friends, and others were the kids that I went to grade school with. They've been unwavering in their support over the years.

Your community and friends are constant and steady reminders, "This is who you are," and as you move through your life, you have the chance to gather an incredible "family" of people from which to learn, with which to share, and with whom to grow. Because they are not personally invested in your business in any way, they also tend to offer fresh perspectives. And if you have a tight knit community, they will check in on you when things are really tough and won't let you isolate. They will notice if you're suddenly quiet or missing from your usual routine, and they will check in on you. It's why it is so important to check in on your strong friends. We tend to go very quiet when we need support, and those that know you will know this. They will have your back and love you through the hard chapters, and in return, when life throws curveballs their way, make sure that you love them and have their backs too.

Gratitude

This one was game-changing for me. I cannot for the life of me remember what first inspired this practice, but I began doing this about eight years ago as a New Year's resolution. I've never been one to give up something for a New Year's resolution. It feels like punishing behavior, and the world can be brutal enough. What I am a fan of doing is adding something positive, a new practice or habit. And one year, my New Year's resolution was to write a letter of gratitude once a week to someone who'd made a positive influence on my life. So I built a spreadsheet and made a list of the people who'd impacted me. It was everyone from family, to friends in this book to a seventh grade teacher who taught me the most effective learning style for my particular brain (Mrs. Haggerty was way ahead of the curve, thank goodness!). It was so powerful, not only writing a list of the recipients, but also sitting down each week with a pen and stationary and going "old school" with a thank-you note. The practice of gratitude was incredible. My grandmother, who lived to almost 108, was a stickler for thank-you notes, so I'd been trained young.

But this time, I was doing it for an entirely different reason, to simply convey gratitude for the people in my life, in my career, and those personally who had wrapped around me during some of my toughest times. I wrote to those I knew well and those I didn't know. I wrote to those who'd taught me, inspired me, encouraged me, and challenged me. And every time I mailed a thank-you note, I heard back. Perhaps because snail mail, handwritten snail mail, is so rare, and perhaps, so is gratitude. But it is so powerful. Again, it has to be true, and it can't be insincere, because that is actually worse. It will require that you get pretty quiet with yourself before you begin to write, to really remember the feelings, the events, the moments, and put those feelings into words. But writing those thank-you notes changed my life. It rewired my brain. Because my focus changed from scarcity to abundance and all of the people and things I had to be grateful for. It began to quiet the negativity and the fear of scarcity, and it began to make those emotions much less tolerable. And it began to change so much internally.

Because when you are operating from a place of gratitude, you cannot also operate from a place of fear. And if you are not operating from fear, but from gratitude and love, it is so much more powerful. Suddenly your governing compass becomes a positive one, and as David Hawkins wrote in *Power vs. Force*, those positive energies are the most powerful. And that shift can end up changing more in your life than you might ever imagine. Gratitude changes grief to grace; it changes grind to grit. It alchemizes so much.

Want to learn more? Robert A. Emmons, PhD, is the world's leading scientific expert on gratitude. He is a professor of psychology at the University of California, Davis, and the founding editor-in-chief of *The Journal of Positive Psychology*. He wrote *The Little Book of Gratitude*.

Faith

In her book, *You've Been Chosen,* Cynt Marshall tells a story that can only be described as one of unwavering faith. She is now the CEO of the Dallas Mavericks and one of the leaders that I admire the most (yes, I sent her a thank-you note!). Her personal and professional lives included obstacles that to some might deem insurmountable. I was given her book by a very dear friend who shared: "You'll read it in one sitting." I did. I could not put it down. It is one of the best books I've read. She is an incredible example of someone with a high FQ score. She was going to figure it out, no matter what the "it" is. I will not spoil the incredible narrative of her story, as it is so very well worth the read, but throughout the book, she shares how she leaned into her faith for so much strength and inspiration. She wrapped herself with it, her community wrapped her in it, her family wrapped her in it, and it clearly held her steady through so many storms. Whatever that faith may be to you, I believe it is a powerful component.

The friend who gave me Marshall's book, which will forever be right up there as one of my favorites, is also the friend who engaged me to give my first TEDx Talk in Austin, Texas, an invitation to share what I'd learned about the food system on the stage. At that point back in 2011, I'd never been in front of an audience that big. When I opened my hotel room curtains that morning, there was a church just below. I said a prayer. When I got to the theater in Austin that day, I was terrified. Pure and complete terror at what I was about to do. I said a prayer, "Let my heart speak." And when I was done, I was so exhausted that I felt like a noodle, and all I wanted to do was to get off that stage, as people began to stand. My thought was, "Thank goodness, there must be a slide that is encouraging a seventh inning stretch or something." Nancy Giordano, the curator of the event, founder of Play Big and author of *Leadering: The Way*

Visionary Leaders Play Bigger, pulled me back on stage. She said, "It's not often that we get a standing ovation like this" and that TEDx Talk went on to be viewed by millions and translated into dozens of languages. That little prayer? "Please let my heart speak." I still say it before absolutely every presentation I give, no matter how big or small the audience. It reminds me of what faith can do.

Want to learn more? Read *You've Been Chosen* by Cynt Marshall. Follow Jay Shetty and Lewis Howes.

Flip the Script

Imposter syndrome. We've all had it. How can we not? We are imposing on systems that are failing us. We are imposing on systems not designed for us or by us. Of course we feel like imposters. We are. We are imposing on a status quo.

A friend of mine, Joe O'Connor, is the president of Applegate, and he candidly shares that he struggled with imposter syndrome. He worked his way through school, and now finds himself at the top of a corporate structure. He recently shared on my podcast, *A Call to Courage*, a story in which he spoke about a conversation on an airplane with a woman sitting next to him, who asked what he does for work. He described his day to day, what he manages, and all that he is responsible for, and she said, "You sound like you're the president or something." He humbly said, "I am."

Imposter syndrome impacts a lot of us. So what can we do when imposter syndrome hits? I've learned to flip the script. Instead of seeing imposter syndrome as a cringe-worthy, triggering thing, see it this way: You are imposing on a system that needs your unique talents, skills, insights, and lived experience. You are also imposing on your fear, which is a seatbelt, holding you back and keeping you strapped in your comfort zone. When you feel like an imposter, don't run the other way. It's actually a compass, an invitation for courage, to break out of your comfort zone and into the magic of living your life at your fullest capacity. If you've put in the work, be brave enough to step toward it. Because I promise you, courage is where the magic happens.

Vulnerability and honesty are strengths because you can't use weaknesses against someone who is already comfortable exposing them.

Imposters? How about change agents and catalysts. We lead, galvanize, expand, and innovate.

As a woman in the finance world, straight out of business school, I got a big dose of imposter syndrome right from the start. I was imposing on a system that was 98% male. I remember touring institutional investors around our trading desk one afternoon, and one of the men asked me if I ever got nervous executing trades. "Would he ask one of the guys this question?" I thought. Then I answered him.

I'd been educated by some of the very best at Rice University's business school. I had an amazing team of colleagues who had my back and are still friends to this day. And the analysis was the same whether the trade was $1 or $100 million. So the answer was, "No. I know what I am capable of, and I know who has my back. I am not nervous recommending multimillion dollar trades."

So the next time you feel imposter syndrome, flip it. Remember your talents and gifts, your innovation and ambition to courageously drive change in the world.

Think about how you want the story of your life to play out. Do you want to be constantly complaining about the people in your life who cut you down? Or do you want to move forward and find those who have your back? Do you want to get to the end of your life and regret that you didn't pursue the life, the purpose that you knew you were capable of? It takes courage to stand up and say, "Enough. We deserve better." And then to create it.

For some reason, something that has always helped me here is to step back and to think of my life like a movie that I am watching.

How do you want that movie to play out? Do you want the main character to stay small? To allow fear to keep you strapped in your comfort zone? Or are you going to pursue life to its fullest?

When I am stuck, I think, "Is this how I want my story to end?" And if it's a terribly hard chapter—and there will be chapters that are so hard, so full of curveballs and pain, that you may feel like you've had the wind knocked out of you—ask yourself, "How do I want this to play out?" Then get to work doing everything you can to build a life that you will be proud of when you get to the end. Impose on the negative chatter in your head, the status quo, and the stale, homogeneous categories.

What do you want your story to be? Have you ever heard about the exercise of writing your own obituary? How do you want *that* to read? Since I lost that dear friend to cancer, I've thought a lot about that. I gave a eulogy at his funeral. I also gave the eulogy at my grandmother's funeral a few years before. Grace, integrity, and love are so important to me. To me, my work is love in action. It always has been. Our lives can be a love story, a love for our families, the planet, each other. How big of a role do you want to give to the naysayers and nonbelievers? Do you want to even give them a role? We all have them in our lives. And how big of a role do you want to give to those who support you and have your back? And importantly, what and who do you want to give your time to? When I think about the things that I want in my obituary, I know that I still have so much more to do.

If that freaks you out too much (and it did me for a while), consider writing your own press release. What would you want to read about in *Forbes*? Or in *Rolling Stone*? Or the *Wall Street Journal*? *GQ* or *Wired*? Write it, print it, and let it serve as your vision board. There will be wild and unanticipated curveballs, for sure, there always are. And there will always be naysayers, but you are the architect of your own life. Take the responsibility seriously. Get intentional about your goals and vision.

Want to learn more? I'd suggest Ken Robinson's book, *The Element: How Finding Your Passion Changes Everything*. It gave me the courage to impose on the systems that weren't designed for our generation and to understand how powerful purpose can be. And listen to Rich Roll's podcast.

Permission to Pause

I will forever be grateful to my dear friend, Aviva Romm, MD, for teaching me this practice. She is a practicing doctor who also has four grown children. We are so careful with what we eat and how much we move, but Dr. Romm also emphasizes how important it is to pause. She calls it "permission to pause" because in our hustle and grind culture, it's hard to stop and get off of the treadmill to recalibrate and regenerate our own energy, purpose, and passion. To stop and to feed ourselves that pause. It is so important. We often feel guilty for taking some time to think, to clear our heads, to pause, but it's one of the most important meetings you can have with yourself. Ideally, you structure this into your weeks so that you aren't forced to pause when something suddenly strikes you down, like illness or disease. It may be five minutes a day, but giving yourself permission to pause, to check in, to breathe, will fuel you and enable you to keep going through all that entrepreneurship throws at you. It helps regulate your nervous system too.

Want to learn more? Follow Dr. Will Cole and check out his site. Watch Reebok's short video, *Permission to Pause*, in which they captured raw home footage featuring Reebok employees and a few of its big brand partners such as Shaquille O'Neal, Conor McGregor, JJ Watt, and Dee Brown, and created a short, heartfelt story of people trying to make the best of a challenging situation, as seen on Jack Morton's website.

Meditation

Like the practice of gratitude, the practice of meditation was absolutely life changing for me. And I say this as someone, who when it first was suggested to me, thought "I'd rather poke my eyes out!" It sounded miserable, and I could not imagine sitting still for 5 minutes, much less 25, with the constant chatter and commotion going on in my brain. But as luck would have it, during a tough chapter of my life, I ended up at a friend's BBQ listening to my friend Alex talk about meditation. He wasn't someone I thought would meditate, so when he shared how it had impacted him, and knowing how similar we are, I took notice. He sent over a few links, and I decided to give it a try.

I am not going to lie, the first week was terrible. I couldn't sit still for longer than about 4 minutes, so trying to get through the 15-minute mediation he'd sent felt like torture, until one day, it didn't. The only thing I can compare that initial meditation to is like when you have to stretch a very tight muscle for the first time. It hurts. There is no flexibility there, and holding that stretch is uncomfortable. That is how it felt to start meditating. And then once my mind actually relaxed into the stretch of it, I started to feel and understand the benefits. It is now a daily practice for me, as important as exercise and brushing my teeth. I feel off when I miss too many days in a row, as it is a way to settle my thoughts, center my emotions, feel my current situation, and then intentionally act from that place. It's been life-changing. When I share the story about how I spoke about the need for this book, then received an email two days later from the team at Wiley Publishing asking if I'd consider writing it, I am often asked if I meditate. Yes, I do, and I will for the rest of my life. It gives you the space to clear your mind and envision the life you want to create.

Want to learn more? My friends at MindBodyGreen.com have some great resources, as do my friends Mallika and Deepak Chopra at the Chopra Center and the Calm App, which you can find on Spotify. The most important thing is to find a practice that works for you. Like exercise, it won't be one size fits all, and there are so many amazing options available to us. Pick one and get started. Don't make the perfect the enemy of the good.

Journal

Have you ever had the experience of meeting a new friend who felt like an old friend? That was the case when I met Darin Olien. You may know him from his work on Shakeology or the Emmy–award–winning series, *Down to Earth with Zac Efron*. Having just lost a dear friend, I was so grateful that the universe sent me a new one. He is someone that I have enormous respect for, in all that he's done, and how he's done it. He has not compromised who he is, and now as the author of *Fatal Conveniences*, he continues to advocate for a safer and healthier life for all of us. He is also the founder of Barukas, a Brazilian-based nut company. He structured the company in a way that honors the land, the people, the farmers, and the integrity of the product. It's a model, much like B Lab, of what is possible. When I sat down with him recently to record his interview on my podcast, *A Call to Courage*, I asked him what advice he would give to someone who wants to bravely step into their next chapter, to stop playing small and expand into all that they can be. His answer? Journal. Start writing, get it down on paper, put the truth out there. He journals every morning, and he shared that the intentionality of writing something down is so powerful for him. I don't know what I expected him to say when I asked that question, but I love this answer.

Every morning, I write down three things that I am grateful for in my journal. Some days, it's easier than others, but again, it's the practice of gratitude (and journaling) that expands your mind into recognizing the abundance of opportunity around you. Some days, it is very simple: a safe home, healthy children, food in the fridge. Some days, it is career focused. Taking the time, every day, to write down what you are thankful for is a great place to start your journaling journey. I also give myself three minutes to write. Every day, that's it. I just let the thoughts pour out. The art of writing is something that you can continue to develop over a lifetime.

What can you do? Pick up a journal, grab an old notebook, open your notes app, and give yourself a few minutes every day (it helps to set a timer) to download your thoughts, express your creativity, share your gratitude, your grief, your frustration, or ambition. It will help you process the thoughts in your head and make your writing stronger.

Music

I am convinced that music is food for the soul. I probably sang before I talked, and no matter the day, no matter the mood, music tends to make things better. I am very grateful to have had very strong musical influences in my life. It was my first passion, and it remains one of my strongest passions today. Again, what we feed our minds matters so much. It's not just the food going into our bodies, but the thoughts and ideas going into our heads. And music can play such a powerful role here. It also can change your brain. According to Johns Hopkins (2109), "If you want to firm up your body, head to the gym. If you want to exercise your brain, listen to music."

There are few things that stimulate the brain the way music does. If you want to keep your brain engaged throughout the aging process, listening to or playing music is a great tool. It provides a total brain workout. Research has shown that listening to music can reduce anxiety, blood pressure, and pain as well as improve sleep quality, mood, mental alertness, and memory.

The team at Hopkins goes on to share, "Experts are trying to understand how our brains can hear and play music. A stereo system puts out vibrations that travel through the air and somehow get inside the ear canal. These vibrations tickle the eardrum and are transmitted into an electrical signal that travels through the auditory nerve to the brain stem, where it is reassembled into something we perceive as music. Music is structural, mathematical and architectural. It's based on relationships between one note and the next. You may not be aware of it, but your brain has to do a lot of computing to make sense of it."

What can you do? Listen to lots of music—your favorites, new music, different genres—head to concerts, find local musicians, teach yourself an instrument, or sing. Music has been so central to my life that I created a playlist for this book called "Creativity." I listened to it on runs when I was writing, and I'd inevitably get home with thoughts in my head that I immediately wanted to download. You can find the playlist on Spotify.

Food

I've written an entire book about this (*The Unhealthy Truth*, 2009), so I am going to keep it super simple here. Fifty-seven percent of the food in the United States is ultra-processed. If you want to think clearly, lead from a healthy place, and feel good, what you choose to put into your body matters. Avoid processed food, cook when you can, eat real food, and cut back on sugary drinks (they're liquid candy bars). Plan ahead. Make sure to bring snacks when you travel; keep a healthy snack in your bag to avoid getting "hangry." Where you can, opt for organic, fresh food. None of us are perfect, so focus on progress. Do what you can, where you are, with what you have. There are loads of resources on this, from the Environmental Working Group, to Civil Eats, to countless books, online resources, and documentaries, like *Common Ground*, featuring Laura Dern, Jason Momoa, and other powerful voices in the food movement, to the Regenerative Organic Alliance on whose board I serve. What you feed yourself matters. Cleaning out the junk in your kitchen is a powerful leadership move. Don't buy the tempting stuff and bring it home. Value yourself for the incredible resource and asset that you are and feed accordingly!

What can you can you do? Read *The Unhealthy Truth*, 2009, watch *Common Ground*, and check out the Environmental Working Group's website.

Get Outside

I can't emphasize this one enough. It changes your perspective, gets you into nature, it's free, it expands your imagination, and it does so much for your mind and body. As little as 15 minutes a day of sun exposure for the vitamin D that is so critical to a healthy body and operating system can do wonders. Again, Andrew Huberman often addresses this on his podcast and Instagram account, urging us outside first thing in the morning. It can help with everything from immunity to sleep to depression. According to an article in *Nature*, "Spending at least 120 minutes a week in nature is associated with good health and wellbeing" (White et al., 2019).

What can you do? Break it down into 15–20 minute chunks each day or do what you can, when you can. Get outside.

Love

I saved the best for last. Don't forget to love. I hope no one needs this reminder, but life gets so busy and can be hard at times, and love is what sees us through. Never miss a chance to tell someone that you love them. It's so expansive. Whether it's a friend, a loved one, a pet, a child, or a family member, I am convinced that love is the most important thing that we can put into the world. It's an incredibly powerful source. Love is a rocket fuel that can inspire us to be braver than we ever thought possible, to do things we never thought imaginable, to build a business, an organization, or a movement that you never thought possible.

"Love in action is service," said Mother Teresa. And like innovation, it changes the world.

Invest in You

I invite you to put these 14 practices to work. I understand how overwhelming entrepreneurship can be, so perhaps choose one practice a month and begin to integrate them into your weekly routine.

Keeping your head and heart clear is an asset to any business model. Your team will benefit, your investors will benefit, and your customers will benefit. As you integrate these practices, your FQ score will increase. You will have resources like creativity, patience, and clarity, which will serve you in your leadership role and in your ability to innovate.

I've found that gratitude is an alchemist. Once you see how the experiences in your life are working for you, teaching you, giving you new skills and relationships, regardless of how hard or easy these experiences may be, you begin to appreciate them. Appreciation for the lessons changes the lens with which you view the world. Gratitude alchemizes the experiences of our lives to grace. Instead of trying to go around the hard times or numb them, you understand that the most powerful thing you can do is to move right through them and collect the wisdom that they hold.

Your life is happening *for* you. Every day is a new opportunity for innovation, courage, and creativity. There is no one else like you, with your unique skills and talents. Where do you want to use them? The landscape of opportunity is wide open, the world needs innovation, and the invitation is clear:

Be brave with your life. It will inspire others to be brave with theirs!

The impact you will make will be felt for generations to come, and no one can do what you are uniquely built to do.

The world needs your unique vision, talents, and authenticity. So do the personal inventory work, find those who have your back. Build your courage, resiliency and supportive scaffolding, and let me know how to help! I would love to feature your story in a future edition of this book! Good luck!

Resources

Johns Hopkins Medicine. (2019). *Keep your brain young with music* [online]. Available at: https://www.hopkinsmedicine.org/health/wellness-and-prevention/keep-your-brain-young-with-music

White, M. P., Alcock, I., Grellier, J., Wheeler, B. W., Hartig, T., Warber, S. L., Bone, A., Depledge, M. H., and Fleming, L. E. (2019). Spending at least 120 minutes a week in nature is associated with good health and wellbeing. *Scientific Reports*, 9(1). Available at: https://www.nature.com/articles/s41598-019-44097-3

A

Your Personal Balance Sheet

THROUGHOUT THE BOOK, at the end of every chapter, I've asked you to make an inventory list.

In one column, you have your positive attributes, your assets. In the assets column are the people, practices, places, and things that you lean on to hold you up, to power you through, to inspire you, and to lift you.

In the other column, you have your liabilities—the naysayers, the nonbelievers, the self-sabotaging behaviors and thoughts, the habits you are ready to lose, the negative thoughts, and anything else that is holding you back, chaining you down, and keeping you from living your innovation.

Your goal is to build your personal assets and minimize your personal liabilities as you move forward. You can use the following chart as a starting point in which to enter your personal inventories.

Keep in mind that as you grow, this list will grow too, both your assets and your liabilities. To keep them in front of you is a strong reminder of your positioning and the strengths you can keep building and the weaknesses and blind spots you can continue to address.

Your Personal Assets	Your Personal Liabilities
Supporters	Shacklers
Healthy Habits	Coping Mechanisms
Network and Community	Isolation Tendencies
Positive Attributes	Unhealthy Behaviors
Additional Assets	Additional Liabilities

B

A 101 on Funding for Startups

As COVERED IN Chapter 9, entrepreneurs will fund their businesses according to their needs, personal financial situation, growth trajectory and other factors. Some of the options available include:

Bootstrapping
Angel Investors
Venture Capital
Crowdfunding
Small Business Administration Loans
Grants

When meeting with those in venture capital, it helps to keep this in mind, as these terms are frequently used:

Funding Series	Typical Capital Raised	Company Stage
Series A	$2 million to $15 million	Early stage
Series B	$10 million to $60 million	Expansion stage
Series C	$20 million to $100 million	Growth stage
Series D	$30 million to $150 million	Late-stage

According to the Founders Network website, other funding options include:

- Working Capital Loans, which provide short-term funding to cover operational expenses, bridge cash flow gaps, or invest in inventory to meet customer demand
- Revenue-Based Financing, which involves raising capital in exchange for a percentage of future revenue
- Merchant Cash Advances, which can be used if your startup generates revenue through credit card transactions and allows you to receive upfront funding based on your future card sales
- Invoice Financing, which is also known as accounts receivable financing and, allows you to receive immediate funding by selling your outstanding invoices to a third party at a discount

Your choice on how you fund your business depends on your company's needs, growth, eligibility, network, and the implications the choices will have on your ownership and control.

Do you want to own the entire thing or share the equity with partners and investors? The answer is not one size fits all. It's a personal decision that impacts not only how quickly you grow your company, but also how you may choose to share ownership, partner with investors, and scale your business.

Source, the Founders Network
https://foundersnetwork.com/blog/types-of-funding-for-startups/

Acknowledgments

To my four amazing children—Lexi, Colin, John, and Tory. The four of you are the most beautiful, courageous souls. Your hearts, intellects, wisdom, intuition, humor, and more inspire me every day. Never doubt for a minute that you hold the entire universe in you, and you are worthy of the deepest love and the most tremendous respect.

To Carrie Cook, the Wiley team, Liz Parks, Alex Bogusky, Erik Bruun Bindslev, Paul Hawken, Katherine Pannill Center, Alison Doering, Meg Siegel, Roni, Zhenya, Fabienne, Meinske, Andrea, Joanna, Peyton, Becky, Dan, Vanessa, Jules, Brooke, Jodi, Chris, Suzanne, and Chris, thank you for the love and support you've shared. I would not be here without you.

To Rose, Holly, Kat, Sarah, Jen, Courtney, Severine, Tina, Seleyn, Gina, Danielle, Shauna, Carla, Julia, Denise, Arlan, Erin, Teri, Nicole, Mariel, Catherine, Michaeline, Roni, Susan and so many other amazing women who now feel like sisters in this work, you inspire me every day, and I feel so lucky to call you friends.

To Robin, Konda, Seanicaa, Mark, and Zach, I am so grateful for your wisdom and friendships.

To my parents, my family, and siblings, thank you for your love and support through so much. To my dad, thank you for always showing me what a passion for entrepreneurship and investing looks like and for modeling integrity, commitment, and patriotism. You are an incredible role model. To my mom, thank you for teaching me strength, humor, and fortitude. Your courageous work in Vietnam with Save the Children has been an incredible example. I would not be who I am without you. To my godmothers, Camille and "Big Rob," you are the truest of blessings, and to my 11 nieces and nephews, being your "Aunt Rob" is one of the best things in life, and I will always work to make the world a safer place for you. And to my Aunt Jenny, you were my first role model of a woman who loved her career, and I have always been so grateful for you.

To the little beach town of Granja, Portugal, your beaches, solitude, and meaning ("farm") provided a beautiful, safe place to create this book.

And to my readers and those on social media who have followed and been with me on this journey from the very start, thank you for being part of this incredible journey and work. You are friends, collaborators, and inspiration. I see you and so appreciate the love and support that you share. We are only just getting started, and I am excited to see what we can do together. The opportunities in front of us are enormous. Thank you so much for your love, support, and courage.

And lastly, this book is written in loving memory of and in gratitude for Chris Van Riet, Suzanne Biegel, Rachel Kranz, my great Aunt Alice, and especially for my grandmothers Mary and Hilda, whose faith, wit, intelligence, beauty, and humor are with me always.

About the Author

ROBYN O'BRIEN was recognized on *Forbes'* Impact 50 list for her work at the intersection of agriculture, food, finance, and climate. She's worked with and presented to companies around the world, including Morgan Stanley, Bloomberg, Bank of America, Rabobank, Target, General Mills, Danone, and Nestlé. She is the founder of Sirona Ventures and rePlant Capital, financial services firms scaling agricultural and climate solutions, and she is a partner at Montcalm TCR, an impact investment firm. After receiving a Fulbright fellowship and graduating as the top woman in her class from business school at Rice University, O'Brien's work in the capital markets began in 1997 at Invesco, where she was on a team that managed $20 billion in assets, launched the company's first hedge fund, and managed the top-performing fund at the company.

She is a best-selling author of the award-winning book *The Unhealthy Truth, How Our Food Is Making Us Sick and What We Can Do About It* (Random House, 2009), and her 2011 TEDx Talk has been viewed by millions and translated into dozens of languages. O'Brien serves on the board of directors of the Regenerative Organic

Alliance, One Green Thing, and other organizations, and she is an executive producer, along with Jason Momoa, Laura Dern, Ian Somerhalder, Rosario Dawson, and others of the award-winning documentary *Common Ground,* about restoring integrity to our food system, produced by Rebecca and Josh Tickell of Big Picture Ranch.

Robyn advises executives at multinational companies, funds, and startups. She is also a sought-after keynote speaker, given her optimism, reputation as a market maker, and ability to capture data, market sentiment, and trends in entertaining narratives and presentations. She is on the board of several organizations and interviews thought leaders and change makers on her podcast, *A Call to Courage*

Robyn is also an adjunct professor at Rice University's Jones School of Business where she teaches a course on innovation and entrepreneurship; she is a cofounder of the conference, Women Transforming Food and Finance; and most importantly, she is the mother of four incredible children who are now navigating the world and its changing landscape.

Index